I JUST WANTED TO GO FISHING!!!

The True Adventures Of Gangster Granny

By
Mary Oyster

© 2004 Mary Oyster. All rights reserved.

No part of this book may be reproduced, stored in a retrieval system, or transmitted by any means, electronic, mechanical, photocopying, recording, or otherwise, without written permission from the author.

ISBN: 1-4140-4169-1 (electronic)
ISBN: 1-4140-4168-3 (softcover)

This book is printed on acid free paper.

1stBooks – rev. 12/30/03

Dedication

For:

Lathan

Officer R. Ryan and the FBI Safe Street Task Force

My Family

Gangster Babies Everywhere

Foreword:

Who the heck is Gangster Granny? Is she a "gangsta" or does she call herself one? If she is one, what kind? There are different types of course such as mobsters, thugs, and garden variety street wanna-be's to name a few. Is it true that she likes to fish, or is the promise of a fishing story just a ploy to get people to read the book? Are there really gangs in Alaska? What is the GTS, and who founded it? What does a "gangster granny" do for a living? And what the heck is a "lick" or some "dirt" anyway?

Have you ever wondered what it must be like to have a gun shoved down your throat so violently that your teeth get knocked out, while you choke so hard on the cold steel that it makes you puke, while pissing on yourself? Hmmm?? Ever wonder what it feels like to have perfectly planned out fishing trips interrupted because of gangsters that do this kind of shit?

The answers to all of these questions and more will be revealed soon! The following pages tell her rather humorous tales of certain experiences leading up to the day her name was changed from just plain old Mary O. to Gangster Granny! Read on. See for yourself. It's all true!

Authors Note:

I wrote this book not only for myself, but because so many people here in Alaska don't realize that we have street gangs up here. I contacted our local newspapers about the gang problem to ask them to do a story on the subject, and when I never received a response, I concluded that somehow I would get the story out. At least the story that my family endured. It is a true account with a few minor exaggerations for humor purposes with some of the names being changed to protect the innocent and not so innocent (whichever the case may be). Is Anchorage "conducive" to *traditional* street gangs? According to a publication dated sometime in the 1990's at *www.uaa.alaska.edu/just/publications/9310gang.html,* Alaska is not at risk. Why? Because it is cold here! This is ridiculous! Nothing is *traditional* (with the exception of Native culture) up here. Every culture must adapt to the environment, and gangs are considered a "culture". The sight should be updated!

The Anchorage Police Department has a pamphlet for the community to read regarding gang activity. One interesting fact mentioned is that most gang members are from 13-21 years of age, with the average shooter being 9-11 years of age. Bet you didn't know that! I believe that this pamphlet should be distributed in all the schools on registration day to the parents to keep them informed. Will the parents read it? Probably not! Besides that, I don't really think that the mayor, current and previous, wants the community to know. It might hurt tourism!

Check this out! My son actually got in trouble in the sixth grade for writing a story about gangs. He knew too much about them. After meeting with the principal and his school teacher, and filling them in on why he knew so much, they decided to let him finish the story. He refused. There are mini-gangsters on the playgrounds. Look around you!!!!!!!!!!!!

It is not hard to join a gang here. You can either get "walked" in or "jumped" in. Getting walked in means that you have become friends with a crew member, maybe have done some drug deals together and are "cool" with other members. Getting jumped in means that you have to do some "dirt" and probably will get the shit kicked out of you. If you are a girl wanna-be, you might have to sleep with all the male gangsters *and* get beat up by the girls. What is "dirt"? Well, it can be robberies, smashing car windows, or anything else that is hideous to show that you have "heart". Get the picture?

Thanks to all of my friends and salon clients who stuck by me through my trials and tribulations with the GTS. Thanks to Officer Ryan and the rest of the "poleece" who did all the work to bust everyone. It is just sad that our justice system doesn't allow for a more speedy outcome. It seemed like it took forever!

United States Attorney's Office
District of Alaska
222 West 7th Avenue, #9
Anchorage, Alaska 99513-7567

FOR IMMEDIATE RELEASE
Thursday, January 31, 2002

Contact: Kevin Feldis
Assistant U.S. Attorney
907-271-5071 / Fax: 271-2345

FIVE MEN INDICTED FOR FEDERAL ROBBERY AND FIREARMS OFFENSES

Anchorage, Alaska - a federal grand jury indicted five alleged gang members on federal robbery and firearms charges stemming from a series of robberies of the Spenard Motel in January 2001. The indictment alleges that Gabriel Clark-Aigner, Timothy Beckett, Raymond Thiele, Daniel Troxel and Crim Alexie conspired together to rob the Spenard Motel and to use and brandish firearms in furtherance of those robberies. As alleged in the indictment, on the 4th, 9th and 30th of January last year one or more conspirators entered the Spenard motel, brandished a handgun, and demanded that the clerk provide all the money from the cash register. Defendant Crim Alexie was shot multiple times during the third attempted robbery.

This case was investigated by the Anchorage Police Department and the FBI as part of a joint state and federal task force focused on reducing violent crime in Alaska. The United States Attorney's Office and the District Attorney's Office coordinated to bring both state and federal charges as part of their efforts to reduce gun violence in Alaska under a nation wide initiative called Project Safe Neighborhoods. In addition to federal charges, these defendants and seven others have been indicted by the State of Alaska as a result of this investigation.

Three of the five defendants will be arraigned in federal court on Friday. They face maximum penalties of 20 years in prison for each robbery charge, and as much as 57 years in prison if convicted of all the firearms offenses.

###

CHARGES ARE MERELY ACCUSATIONS; AND DEFENDANTS ARE PRESUMED INNOCENT UNTIL PROVEN GUILTY AT TRIAL OR A PLEA OF GUILTY IS ACCEPTED BY THE COURT.

Table of Contents

1	A Day At The Salon	1
2	King of the Camp!	10
3	Fish Tales Get The Truth!	18
4	I Just Wanted To Go Fishing!!!	24
5	Cats, Guns, & Inbreds!	42
6	Chillin' Wit' Da' Feds!	48
7	Yo! Big Daddy!	61
8	Movers, Treasure & Stuff	65
9	Watchin' Our Backs	71
10	Gangster Granny!	75
11	Da Phone Iz Ringin'!	91
12	Court Full Of Gangsters!!	97
13	Hangin' Wit' My Homefry!	108
14	Writings From The Big House!	119
15	Yo! Da End Of Da Story	135

Chapter 1

A Day At The Salon

On a typical day at the nationally renowned (at least in some circles) Mercury Studio, I get there around 9:00am. I like to get there early so as to avoid the huge cluster of the other hairdressers/stylists rushing to the coffee pot before the first client comes in. I like it when it is quiet there because I can maybe remember exactly why I really wanted my own hair salon. It certainly wasn't because I wanted the added drama or financial headaches in my life - although it is rather humorous hearing about the latest success story from the girls regarding an evening of stalking certain available "boys". The financial headache more than likely will never end, so I am pretty much stuck with it.

Anyway, morning there for me also (at least now) means that when I look down upon the street I don't have to worry about the *gangsters*. They are all in bed after a fine night of robbing people (doing licks), ingesting various drugs and plotting retaliation for crimes against them. They're certainly not tired after a midnight run to the fishing hole, which is why I would be tired.

I have assembled a fabulous crew of hairstylists. I won't mention any given names but they include a bouncy, bubbly, loud mouthed young woman, who has a huge heart and who fancies herself petite. This stylist is working on perfecting her body, and so eats nothing but protein pudding, protein bars, protein shakes, and to stir things up a bit some watery chicken soup. She moonlights as a cocktail waitress at a house of ill repute (girly bar), and she dreams of one day having hair so long and luxurious that she can style it into "stripper" hair. She is also our Salon Manager and tires easily of my endless stories about fishing and gangsters. She has no stereotypical set of clients who are attracted to her for whatever reason. For the most part they are from all walks of life. (except lowlife's) Lot's of male clients and lots of the young party crowd. Her name is Hoochie Mama.

Our Assistant Manager is a tiny thing who happens to be extremely neurotic, and will on occasion cry for no apparent reason. She is very fidgety and flighty, and upsets easily, therefore throwing the poor receptionists into fits of terror at the thought of this tiny stylist running behind. I have been told by my Fishing Partner that I should go easy on her, as she is quite fragile emotionally. The mention of this throws our first stylist into fits of laughter. Tiny is our official "boy" stalker and has only managed to enslave her conquest once after burning him with a cigarette. Other than that, she is very sweet and also dreams of having luxurious hair, as she was cursed with course pubic-like hair which she straightens out with great care and lots of products. Her clients are mostly Girdwoodian's, which are hippy-ish in looks and thinking. We have never figured out why she has attracted them to her. Maybe it is for her long winded stories within stories within stories. We shall never know. She also has some professional people. She too tires of my fishing and gangster stories, but listens to them with patience........ Her name is Tiny.

Our third girl is a very slim little thing with a sweet personality, who is always under my wing craving approval. (Hoochie thinks approval craving is a brown-nosing technique.) She actually likes to hear my stories about gangsters and fishing because she thinks them funny. This stylist probably would cry if I teased her too much, so I am careful of how I say things. She doesn't care if she has luxurious hair or not, and I can certainly appreciate that because I too have no use for luxurious hair. I like when she does her impression of Doctor Evil from the movie Austin Powers. It is perfect, and sometimes laughing at it gives me a stomach ache. She is planning on becoming a famous dancer and dreams of being in a Janet Jackson video, or maybe dancing for J.Lo. Her clients are a mixed bag of fun middle aged lady's who *let her know* that they *are* getting older, and young guys and a few young girls who want to be *really cool.* They all think she is The Best Hairdresser. Her name is Lil' Dancer.

Our fourth stylist is a guy who is straight (at least I think) who is only twenty four years old, married with four kids. He dreams of becoming a famous stylist to the stars or at least a platform artist, (platform artists are just regular hairstylists who work for a product company, who have elevated themselves above all other stylists because they work on a stage) or educator (same thing as a platform artist except in a salon). He also would like to work for the cosmetic company MAC. He is a conservative yet wanna-be-flashy stylist who can twirl his shears like a pistol (it makes his clients think that he can do great hair) and he cuts himself on a daily basis. He shows these cuts to me every day as does the last stylist. I am supposed to admire that because I told both of them that if they weren't bloody from a new technique, then they simply weren't challenging themselves. Pretty funny. Anyway, he is the sort of person who is late every day and drives to church on flat tires without realizing why he feels thumping....... He is very schmoooozy and so attracts the forty-five plus crowd who think they are very glamorous when in actuality they are nothing more than older women with low self esteem who happen to have loads of money. (They also carry around twenty year old photo's of themselves so that they can remember when....) We call him Schmoozy.

I am stylist number five. I am probably an oddball to some people because I don't usually agree with all mainstream ideas for one reason, plus I change my hair color on a weekly basis, and I prefer to wear giant shoes. Some people are disappointed when they meet me since I am not as "wild" as they expected from the description given them from the referring client. I love everyone that I work with which will probably be the downfall of my salon. More than likely the downfall will come from not having much of a business mind, although I try new tactics every day. Anyway my clients are a wide variety of people over thirty who like to hear my stories, think I am a Hair Goddess and love to come to the salon for a laugh. I have gained fifty pounds since Halloween, (due to all the steroids that I have either ingested or had injected into me) from all the asthma attacks I have had from the stress of being haunted by gangsters when I should have been fishing. *I never would have thought gangsters were a big deal until my daughter became one*. She would have been stylist number six had I not fired her sorry ass! .

Now that I have familiarized everyone with the stylists, I will say a short piece about the salon. My husband Big Daddy tired of hearing me whine about owning my own salon so he renovated two places for me in three years. The first one was definitely not as busy as this new one. The one we are in now is located in a really cool old building across from the Nordstrom's on *The Corner* of downtown Anchorage. A short bit up the street is the transit center where the gangsters like to hang out. I like to watch them from one of the windows. Anyway, Big Daddy slaved for two months on it, and it is truly glorious. There are archway doors, concrete floors, chain link shelves and big arched windows. Mercury Studio stylists hate perms and everything to do with perms and we avoid them at all costs. We do color and haircutting. I have a "shrine" in the corner dedicated to all my fishing gifts that clients give to me. My newest addition is a ceramic tic-tac-toe fishing game. All my clients know that I love to fish and some of them have even been canceled because of a large run of fish. They do not mind this because they know that it makes me happy, and they will have a fine story. Plus some of my finest hairdo's and colors have been inspired from the river!

For some interesting salon trivia, I will mention here that for some reason, all hairstylists are obsessed with lunch. Lunch? Doesn't everyone who works get lunch? Well, the answer to that would be NO!, unless you happen to work at a regular nine to five desk job. Lunch at a hair salon starts with someone mentioning around 10:30am that we should all *think about lunch.* Around 11:10am certain stylists start noticing that there stomachs *might* start rumbling soon. For them, it's not about what sort of glorious hairdo's they might do that day, it is all about when they will get to eat lunch. They can almost taste the curly fries, or sub sandwiches, or cheap Chinese take-out! The panic sets in around 12:00pm. They just know that there will be no time for lunch. So they rush out the door in between haircuts for a pretzel, and guess what, the next client no-shows for the appointment and the poor sad stylist is too full of squished up pretzel to be hungry for anything else. But since the No Lunch Panic has already grabbed a firm hold, he or she might run up anyway for a full-on lunch, inhale it quickly, bitch because they feel sick, and then do it again the next day. This could possibly explain why there are so many chubby hairstylists in Anchorage.

Anyway, now that I have introduced you to everyone except the receptionists, (they both will be a mere memory by the time I am done telling this story) let us start the day! Here come the clients. Some are just waking up. Some have never been to bed, and they all want coffee. The Girdwoodian's however, prefer Chai Tea of some sort with cream rather than coffee. They all also know that there isn't any such thing as decaffeinated anything at Mercury either. The worst is when they show up early and *we* haven't even had our coffee.... Especially Tiny. Whew!

It's August 15, 2001, and it is a beautiful day. (remember this date because I will be caught telling stories within the story, sorta like Tiny who does that alot). I start my day as I would any other work day - make coffee, drink some coffee, count the till, print the reports, assemble the reports, turn on the music, wait for everyone and look at my day's schedule. Hopefully I would have a full day so as to avoid the time consuming chore of writing out the hateful bills. *"Hmmm.. Let's see, who is my first client? Excellent, it is Mable from Fairbanks, someone that I like. And Dorrinda! Most deluxe! Everyone on the books today will be fun!"* Here come the stylists and here come the clients. All at the same time I might add. Hmmm....

"Hello Mable. How are you today?" I ask as I lead her over to my station. Not that I really cared, I was still having some issues with the incidents of the day before, which I will get into shortly. We went through our normal conversation that we always have about her hair. No more than an inch cut off, just a color touch up, no styling wax for the finished hairdo, etc. All of which I already knew, it's just something we always have to say. Then it was her turn to ask questions.

"Well Mary, how is your daughter Ray-Ray doing? Is she still over at the other salon? How does she like it?" Mable asked. I could hear from across the room Hoochie shouting that Mable *didn't want to know*! I could hear Tiny over in the corner reprimanding Hoochie Mama for eavesdropping, and I could hear Lil' Dancer breathing with the anticipation of a fine story. Meanwhile Schmoozie still hadn't even arrived. Probably another flat tire or something.

"Well Mable, you remember that I sorta disowned her last on my birthday, right? Remember? She was being a freak and hanging out with the white trash. You know, the creepy, nasty in-breds with greenish teeth?" I asked. She said that she did remember that I was complaining about that during her last visit.

"Ok. Well yesterday I found out that she was pregnant after I called her to tell her that we had to put Riverman to sleep." I replied. Riverman was one of the family dogs that we had for many years. We got him from a girl whose husband had rescued him and all his brothers and sisters the day he was born. His mother was a prize winning Mastiff and she got knocked up by a Black Lab, so the owner being ashamed of that, was going to put all the puppies to sleep. So this couple bottle fed all the puppies and gave them all away. I named him Riverman because my plan was that when he was older he would help me land all the giant fish that we had caught.

Anyway, I went on to explain to Mable how Riverman was overly protective at the house, and the camp, but NEVER any other time. About how he has attacked other dogs before, and how I had turned my deck into a kennel to keep him in if we weren't home. He was quite the jumper of fences so that is what I had decided to do. Anyway, the Sunday before that he had bolted out the door, (I was getting the kids some Burger King) and jumped one of those wrinkle dogs. He made quite a mess of that dog, so naturally his owner was very angry. He was backed up by a pack of geriatric neighbors (Gerries) who were determined that I would not escape when I returned from Burger King. To make a long story even longer, after paying the vet bill, hiding River from the dog pound, and crying alot, the kids and I took him to our family veterinarian, and we bid him farewell as he went to sleep one last time. I determined for everyone that when he got to Heaven (as all dog's do) that there would be plenty of bad dogs there that he could chase. That made us all feel a little bit better anyway.

"So how did your daughter take the news?" Mable asked.

"Well, she took it so well, and thought I was taking it so well, that she figured that she should go ahead and inform me that after a whole summer of not talking to each other, she was pregnant." I said. "And I'm like, well how the Hell did that happen? Besides the obvious. And she says she was too broke to get the pill and so I say, **HELLO!** Babies cost a helluva lot more than the pill! Are you gonna have it? Who is the father? Do you know who the father is? Are you getting married? What is the deal? Are you happy? How can you be happy? Are you even more of a dumbass than I thought?" And so it went for the rest of my tirade.

I filled her in on how in the course of one day, (August 14th) I put my dog to sleep, made posters for all the neighbors announcing the fact, and then found out that I was going to become a Grandmother. What a day that was to forget! Gee whiz........ by the time I was done with that story, I was done with Mable's hair. And, although I was a bit negative during the service, it was quite a fine hairdo I must say. She paid the bill and gave me a hug as lots of my clients do. I was certainly tired that day after telling the story over and over again. And the stylists all were ready for me to be done with the story.

The day's end at Mercury is pretty much the same as the beginning. Except that while the reports are printing, the coffee is getting dumped and everyone scurries around cleaning (or pretending to clean) and then Tiny and Hoochie pretty themselves for whatever the evening ahead may hold. More than likely Tiny will talk Hoochie into going out with her to look for cute boys. Poor little Tiny, she has one boy who might wait forever for her. Lil' Dancer will be off to teach dance lessons, and Schmoozie will go home to his family. I too will go home to the family, family who are supposed to be tying some flies.

Big Daddy came home from hunting that week, and before I could tell him all the bad news about Ray-Ray, the kids beat me to it. He says that is why he likes to work away from home. There is too much drama here. Which is true, so, off we went to the fishing hole for some much needed fun. I have to fish every weekend in the summertime. It is what keeps me sane. Always has been. Always will be.

I Just Wanted To Go Fishing !!!

Plus it is good for the kids. Even when they are tired of fishing, they still want to come with me to hang out. And believe me, once Labor Day is here, they are pretty well tired of fishing. The only real amusement for them by then is making fun of Mother as she trips over Trick Rocks, and Secret Roots while in a frenzy to get to the fishing hole.

Chapter 2

King of the Camp!

Like Mable, all of my clients know that Memorial Day weekend is my favorite time of year. You see, Memorial Day is usually my birthday, and it is always the start of King Season, and all fishing in general, at least as far as I am concerned. So at night as I lay in bed thinking about the days events, my thoughts would always wander to fishing and the weekend coming up. What kind of cool stuff I would get for my birthday. How many fish I would catch with my birthday presents.... (I always get camping and fishing stuff. One year I got a fly rod from a fishing buddy we sometimes call Camp Dad. That particular present caused tears of choked up joy to flow down my dirt and campfire crusted cheeks.) The hopes that the kids would catch fish. How big of a bonfire I would make - that sort of stuff. I start thinking about these things along about February. I think about them so hard that I end up tossing and turning all night long due to the raging fishing dreams that I have. I have dreams that I can see huge fish rolling and I can't get to them. Or

I Just Wanted To Go Fishing !!!

I have hooked one at least 80 pounds and every time I get it to the bank the line breaks. Or I am chasing one down the river and I keep falling down. (I fall down alot when I am fishing, because I don't pay much attention to the Trick Rocks and Secret Roots that are continually jumping up to catch the tips of my boots. I have been named the Bumble Master because of this.) I have even flung myself right off the bed chasing a fish! So I have been told by Big Daddy. Some mornings I wake up more tired out than when I went to sleep!

Anyway, I close the salon every Memorial Day weekend so I can't be called back for some disaster. Like the time I was gone and we had a flood at the salon. I just happened to call them in between fish to find out that they couldn't figure out what plumber to call, for fear that I would get mad if it was the wrong one! I decided right there and then, I would never call the salon again while out fishing! Plus all the stylists like getting extra days off although great fun is poked at me for the Mercury Studio Fishing Holidays.

Let's back track a bit. The Thursday before Memorial Day 2001 started pretty much as any other Thursday before Memorial Day. Get to the salon, make the coffee, print the reports, check the messages, wait for the stylists etc. Answer the phone and inform one of Schmoozy's clients that he no longer worked at Mercury since I was in the Firing Mood awhile back. Gaze out the window up the street towards the Gangsters Hangout, wishing it was time for me to leave for the Anchor River. Wishing it was time to get in the Fish Mobile with the kids and dogs and HEAD OUT! This year would be different though. Big Daddy wouldn't be there because he was working on some rich guy's cabin across the bay, and I was not including my oldest daughter Ray- Ray this year because she had become somewhat of a weirdo by hanging out with the white trash, and we're talking T-rash! Everyone else would be asking where she was, and what would I tell them? That I couldn't be around her because she was throwing her life away? That I was more interested in catching the biggest fish than trying to get through to her? Maybe I would just say that she had to work. Wish those stylists would get here..... This is what they do. Make me wait so when I am done with the opening chores, I am left to ponder too many things.

Finally after what seemed like hours, the stylists all rolled in along with the assortment of one Girdwoodian, one hockey mom, one neurotic fur wearing forty five year-plus Nordstrom shopper, one Nordstrom employee, and one shoe store owner. The shoe store owner is my client who has been with me at every salon I have ever worked at. She will be loyal till the end of my career or whenever her hair falls out, whichever comes first. She has heard all of my fishing story's, seen my kids as they have grown, heard all the drama's and stories of my days as a cocktail waitress... You get the picture.

"Hey! How's it goin' Cindy? Bring yourself on over here and have a seat." She comes over after visiting with the receptionist for a minute. She always visits with whatever receptionist we happen to have. She is good like that. Her hair was looking rather faded this particular day because I no-showed on her the week before due to some drama from Ray-Ray. (She had gotten fired from a hair job that I procured for her, after I fired her for partying too much and being late all the time. I had co-signed her a truck and had to take it back from her) Anyway, she sits down like she always does. Tiny comes over and pets her on the shoulder like she always does with every client on her way over to her own client. Hoochie Mama shouts a good morning like she always does. Lil' Dancer of course flitted past us like a graceful swan, only to trip over the shelf as she does once or twice a week I was happy to be doing her hair that day. She has a short red hair hairdo that I am rather proud of, has a spunky personality, four kids, and weighs about 80 pounds because she runs around like a chicken with her head cut off chasing kids, employees and customers while her husband is out hunting, or doing important business with the Russians. (I know that last one is a run-on sentence, but that is how it is.)

She asked if I was going fishing. As if! Of course I was. In fact I was only doing *her* hair and then I was GONE! GONE!!! GONE FISHING!!!! I had to fill her in on my dumb-ass daughter, the whereabouts of Big Daddy, my pets, my *little* kids, my birthday wish list, and who all were going to the Anchor Festivities, etc... Would I be fishing at midnight on Friday? Damn right. Would I be making a bonfire! Oh yes! (I made one so big that the Sideways Rain evaporated before landing on us, and that is no lie! I got to burn up six truckloads of wood that weekend. Big truckloads! It was so righteous! My Fishing Partner brought a truckload, and Big Daddy had cut up one truckload for us that My Fishing Partner was instructed to inform me to "make it last the whole weekend", heh heh heh heh heh ......) Do the kids still like to fish? Well yes. Would I be bringing the oldest daughter? That would be a BIG NO. Was I closed for the weekend? Of course. Whew! So many questions! So little time to answer them! I had to go! Fish On!

So after the two hours of hair wizardry, and my What I Was Going To Do This Weekend story, I was gone. Free at last! Free to go score the campsite on the beach for the "village" that I would make for all the friends. My biggest concern would be whether or not I would get stuck in the sugar sand in the Fish Mobile. That had happened to me the last Memorial and one of the boat-launch tractors had to pull me out which cost $25.00 and a good dose of embarrassment plus a few choice cuss words.

What is the Fish Mobile? Well, since you asked, I'll tell ya. It's a beautiful 1973 Dodge motor-home with a giant fish painted on the side. (The fish mural was painted on it as a gift from Ray-Ray two or three summers before this one when she was of sound mind.) I got it for one Alaska Permanent Fund Dividend, some haircuts, and around $1,000.00 in cash. I am not certain of the exact amount. All

Mary Oyster

I am certain of is that Big Daddy continually says that it was more than that, which I have no recollection of. Hmmmm. At any rate, I thought it a fine car, and was immensely happy driving it. The Happy Car. (I called it that once in front of My Fishing Partner, and he assured me that talk like that could send me to the psychiatric ward for some treatment and medication.) I wasn't very happy about that, and figured that I should keep my personal feelings about the Fish Mobile under tight wraps. Anyway, it was also a gathering place for all the Memorial Day beach campers and was famous for the extra stiff coffee, camping potatoes and breakfast. Mmmm Mmmmm. I can smell it now!

Midnight on Friday of Memorial Day Weekend is a big deal symbolically. It's sorta like having fireworks for the 4th of July! The anticipation of the first cast, of the first shout of FISH ON!! We all put on our waders and wait. Everyone's eyes are on the water, which is usually already at high tide which sucks because there is no drift. But we don't care, we are all just happy to be there, waiting for fishing season to begin. And every year it is the same for me. I just know that *this* year will be the year that *I* will have the first 50 pounder on the bank! At the very least, I would have the first one on!

I had been skunked for kings the last year, so of course I was extra impatient. I was so excited that when midnight finally arrived, all I could do was fling my line across the river, entangling the other guy. *Shit!* Next cast. Plunk! *Damn it calm yourself...* Next cast. *Perfect.* The familiar tapping along the bottom was even more exciting. And then WHAM! *Wahooo! FISH ON!!!* I set that hook like nobody's business! I would chase that fish out to the ocean and wrestle it, and gill it, and then carry it back for all to see! Wahooo! I had plans for that fish. But no! What's this?! The fish wasn't moving! I was sure I had a fish. No! No! No! It couldn't be! It was a Wiggly Tree laying there, out to grab my line and make me think I had a fish on! The guy next to me did! *That's not right! I was supposed*

I Just Wanted To Go Fishing !!!

to have the first fish on! Me! Me! Me! Now the Fish Panic was setting in. I had told myself that this year would be different. This year I would remain calm. (Big Daddy absolutely hates fishing with me because I'm so excited. Says that I ruin the event for everyone because of it.) But no! My mind struggled with the Fish Panic as the rest of me struggled to free the hook from the snag. Yank, yank, yank! Snap! It was free at last! But alas, my hook was left behind in the depths of the river. That was ok because I didn't like that set-up anyway. What I really wanted to use was a glow-in-the-dark bead. By the time I re-rigged, it was slack tide and the festivities were over. Just like last year! So back to the bonfire we went, just like every year. And like every year, I ponder whether or not to sleep with my waders on....

The next day after breakfast, and fishing the outgoing tide, we gather up our gear and head off to the Ninilchik River. All must go, or they will miss out! So after sleeping in the waders (they are Gortex and come with another story, which by the way had become rather snug on me (due to some asthma/steroid weight gain) off we go. After several moments of Fish Panic, and several close calls with Wiggly Trees, YES!, I did catch the first king! When I did, I yelled for all to hear that I was King of the Camp! I reefed that fish right on in on my 8 weight. Whew what a fight! Heh heh heh.... How big was it? Well, some people say that it was a nothing but a small jack, I say it was at least 30 pounds. The pictures say that it was smaller than a silver. I say throw away the photo! Now I am known as The King, or just plain King. What is even worse, I often answer to it.

While I was busy being The King at the Ninilchik, a much larger fish was being pulled out of the Anchor by my second daughter. At Fishing Camp she is called Wiggly Tree because she catches lots of them. Her real name is Bunkie. Anyway, she had hooked a 35+ pounder in the back and managed to horse it on in. I found this amazing because firstly it is definitely hard to land a foul-hooked fish that big, and secondly the river was way high and moving fast. Being the law abiding fisherman that she is, she went to release it after all her hard work. While figuring out the best way to unhook the fish, a fellow fisherman (adult) asked her if she was Mary's daughter, and why she would release such a fine fish after wrestling it to shore. She of course confessed that *yes* she was my kid, and that she *had* to release it because it was *snagged*. To which the man said that he would keep it if he was her, and then he netted it ant carried it to camp for her. I still don't know who that guy was although everyone says I do, and that he is a friend of Camp Dad's. So just imagine my embarrassment when I got to camp bearing the name King, just to discover that my fish was smaller than half of hers! I should have thrown it back!!!!!

The weekend after Memorial Day is usually a better king weekend. And since we all go fishing every weekend we went. But for some reason for which I have no explanation, I became paranoid of crossing the river although I had crossed it many times in the same spot. I do not know what happened last year, I just know that I couldn't (wouldn't) cross the river. My Fishing Partner became rather disgusted after demonstrating several times how easy it was, and left me there. Ditched me, he did! Actually if the truth be known, I said that I was going to find a better spot to cross. After discovering that I couldn't find a better spot, I found a nice log to sit and pout on. There I sat, feeling sorry for myself for my paranoia. I *just knew* that for some reason my Fishing Partner had ditched me. I figured that he couldn't stand to be around me that day because maybe I was too depressed about Ray-Ray (who was still hanging out with the white trash and not working. She was on her way to becoming a gangster, only I didn't know it yet). I pondered on her for awhile and got myself all worked up into an emotional *girl mood*. Good grief! I couldn't figure out what happened.! So then I became angry with myself and determined that I would cross that river. What in the hell was the matter with me!?!?

After reaching the crossing spot once again, I changed my mind. I don't know why. I can't figure it out. It doesn't matter though, because if I would have crossed the river, I never would have taken the kids to the "Flounder Hole", where the Jumble Master (my son-his real name is Buddy) caught his first king. It was a fine king too!

The Flounder Hole is pretty close to the mouth of the river, and we named it that because flounders are pretty much all you can catch there. The kings just speed on through that spot. So we sat there, blobs of eggs laying there 2 feet from the bank. Waiting for flounders. Kicked back, just hanging out when all of a sudden, I saw the forty plus pounder rush Jumble's bait and grab it. I shouted for him to SET THE HOOK! SET THE HOOK!, and he was yelling HOW? and I shouted for him to REEF ON IT! REEF ON IT! YANK IT! YANK IT! And reef he did! The fight was long and exciting to watch. He kept getting jerked into the river. The tide was coming in too, so the danger of that added to the excitement. Finally the fish was becoming tired and I told Jumble to turn him. Which he did, and when it came close to me I wrestled him outta the water and stabbed him in the head. The tide was coming in quick now, and we needed to get out of there. It was tough. That fish did not want to become dinner! After dispatching it with a knife stab to the brain, that fine fish was carried and dragged back by the Jumble Master to the Bronco winning praise from all who saw it.

My Fishing Partner caught a big Anchor king that day too and we all had a fine bar-B-Q with beans which we always have with salmon. He was still disgusted by my failure to cross the river, and to this day teases me about being a *girl* even though I am one.

Chapter 3

Fish Tales Get The Truth!

Back at the salon, every day is the same when masterminding a fabulous hairdo. Different clients. Different day. Some people want to look "just like the picture" (these ladies will show you every time the photo that they have been carrying around for decades). Some clients want the exact replica of a haircut that a stylist gave them 20 cuts before this one. Like we can remember that far back! Some people want a change but want to keep the length. (HELLO! You can't make a change without cutting the hair! What is that anyway??) Some people want to look older. Some people want to look thinner. Some older clients want to look younger but don't want to color the hair, want to wear it long, no fringe but want it to frame the face. Some folks don't want layers but want height. Yeah right! Do you know that most people who wear long hair complain of it getting in their face, so they wear the Forever Ponytail? Let the ponytail down and cut it off if all you're going to do is wear a ponytail! Cut the shit off or quit complaining!!! Or better yet, go fishing and calm yourself.

Or here's another one. Client comes in. Wants chunky hilites and then complains about it looking like stripes. What in the hell do they think *chunk hilites* are?!?!? Big chunks or small chunks, they are still freaking stripes!

Or how about the ones who tell us how to color the hair? Or go on for hours about how this one time this stylist at the most expensive salon in LA did her hair, and that no one can do it the same chunky way! For the LOVE! Or how someone 10 years ago gave her the most hideous color in beauty school and now she doesn't trust anyone. HELLO! You went to a Beauty School! School is where you get your hair jacked up so the students can learn how to fix it! I'll tell ya what! What if I want to make your hair a spawning salmon color? - (Crimson with a touch of fuchsia overlay with deep burgundy undertones) *What about what color I want to make?* It will look nice! I swear! Ah well, I do realize that no one but me would appreciate salmon colored hair........... Plus I do get paid to do really boring hair....

Or what about women who are so stuck in the early 80's that they still believe crap about being a Winter? What is a Winter? Well, I wouldn't know. I do know however, that people who see themselves as a "season", can only wear certain colors. Or not wear certain colors depending on their "color palate". Hmm... I wonder who made a bazillion dollars off of that idea! Also, people who are of this group tend to be extremely neurotic, and question every snip of the hair, and every move you make with the brush. Very annoying. I could write an entire chapter about this group, but I will save that for another book.

Or how about the people who lie about their hair? Lie about going to someone else who screwed up their hair, and then try and say it was one of us who did it? As if we don't know our own haircuts! Most people who fib about this (to me anyway) will usually confess after I have told a few fishing stories to them. Especially the stories about Midnight Fishing Power Runs which are done on a weekly basis

Mary Oyster

throughout the summer. Power Run?

All true Alaskan's (at least salmon chasing ones who live around Anchorage) know what a Power Run or Suicide Run is. But since you asked.... It's super quick *run* down to the river in a *powerful* fast rig (to shave off those few minutes of driving) done right after work. To go on a proper Power Run, you must have all of your gear previously thrown (not packed) into the vehicle of choice. Your fishing partner for Midnight Runs must be chosen carefully. They *must* like the adrenaline rush of the fast driving necessary to get there. Speeds under 80mph are unacceptable. They *must* be able to withstand lack of sleep. They *must* not be wimpy. My Midnight Power Run fishing buddy is a chick named Daizy. I chose her not for her fishing ability (she can't catch a fish to save her life), but because she is always ready for adventure, and is the only person who truly appreciates my wondrous driving, and abilities to acquire parking space in the Combat Zone. Plus she doesn't have a fit when she gets skunked. Which is pretty much always.

So anyway, here I was at the salon in mid June, quite disgusted at my client Donna for outright bullshitting me about her hairdo. She had secretly colored her own hair at home a nice greenish tone, totally against my professional advice, and then went to another salon to have it fixed so that she could possibly pass it off to me as something I did. Why? Why? Why?!?!? What does she take me for? Stupid?! Don't these people realize that by trying to save a buck they end up spending hundreds of dollars to fix it? Whatever.. Ok. Go to the back. Clear off the counter Hootchie's left over mess.   Mix the fix... So while mixing her color remover, I couldn't help thinking about the great fishing adventure Daizy & I had the night before. Just two purty gals, out to catch a fish.........

"So ask me how many fish I caught last night Donna!" She already had been informed that I was feeling festive because I had caught lots of reds. She of course asked if I had been fishing, like a good client would - she was hoping that I

wouldn't give her a hard time about her color. She also inquired about Daizy.

"*Well Donna, are you sure you want to hear the story? I caught assloads of fish! Piles of them! But first let me tell ya. If you want a good parking spot just bring some beer.*" Feeling quite pleased with myself with the questioning look on her face I went on to explain how the young, out of state, Fish & Game workers at the booth asked if we "trade". "*Sure, what sort of trade?*" That night I was feeling some major Fish Panic so I would have traded pretty much anything right then for him to let us through. Quickly I had surveyed the front seat. Beer for Daizy, chips for us, soda pop for me, Reeses Peanut Butter Cups for her. Some M&M's. Hmmm. Daizy, being the good buddy that she is, quickly handed it all over. I told the guy if that wasn't enough he could have her too. At which she smacked me soundly. We were IN that day and every other day after that! Doin' some trades!

"Anyway, after I was done catching fish, and Daizy was tired of trying, we left for home. First a quick stop at Gwin's Lodge for coffee and we were on our way. I wanted to be in bed by 2:00am since I had to get up at 6:00am. Of course the needle was buried until we rounded the bend at Girdwood where the Girdwoodian's live. Plus cops like to catch speeders there, and you just plain have to slow down. That, and shortly thereafter, the road becomes twisty and narrow so we are forced to drive responsibly anyway. It's those last 30 miles that take forever too. I wanted to take care of my fish before catching more - I was already planning on going again the next night. I would have to get another buddy to go with me though, cause Daizy, who was busy sleeping, had to work. Hmmm.. As I was pondering these important things I noticed a white truck or Bronco coming on us quick. That jerk-wad was on my ass! He was swerving too. "*Daizy! Wake up! Look at this jerk! He is going to run into us!*" She yells to let him pass and so I slowed down and pulled over. He slows down, pulls up next to us, and won't pass. So I decided to speed up and lose him. So he is right on my ass again! So

I slow down again! Then he slowed down and sort of pulled over to the side. We get up around a bend and are relieved that he is gone."

"All of a sudden he is back, hauling ass, and on our tail. Then he shuts off his lights, swerves around us. and up next to us There was this big semi coming towards us in the other lane. *The lane the freaks were in.* Only the semi didn't know that the white bronco was in his lane 'cause it's lights were off. I slowed way down & we were like - Oh My God!, and then the jerk flips his lights on to freak out the semi driver who almost takes him out before he whips into our lane ahead of us. *"Shit! What an asshole!"* So then, he slams on his brakes to wait for us to catch up. Daizy is yelling for me to just pull over, and I am thinking NO FREAKIN' WAY! So then he plays his light trick in some more oncoming traffic, and then this time slams on his brakes and whips in behind us this time and then speeds up and rams into my car (it's a Bronco but I call it a car). Not once but twice he hits us. He is totally trying to run us off the road where they are going to plan unmentionables upon us! Daizy is still yelling for me to pull over cause she doesn't want to die due to car crash, while I don't want to die of murder or whatever the psycho boys have in store for us. He gets in front of us one more time and speeds up, slows down, speeds up, slows down. So I am MAD and I speed up to get his license plate. Flip on the brights, Daizy writes down the plate, and the passenger waves something out the window back towards us. Daizy yells it might be a gun, so I slow down one last time hoping that he will speed up and go away. But No!!!!"

"Shit! He was slamming on his breaks again! FOR THE LOVE! We were pretty much fucked at that point. I figured that these guys wanted to rape us or murder us or both. There was no way that was going to happen to me. I would die in a fiery crash first! But I knew that God wanted me to get home, He just wanted to test my driving skills. (you see, it has been said by my Fishing Partner, that my car was a death trap because of the way the front end shakes - except at high speeds) So, after hearing a voice (God's I figured) saying "My Car Is Not A Deathtrap", I yelled for Daizy to HOLD ON! I was losing these bastards! So, pedal to the metal, we blasted around those guys, side hopping at 75mph on the winding road. The fish were flopping all over the back, surely laying fish slime and scales everywhere. Big Daddy would not be pleased with that, that was for certain, but I would have to think about that later. Those guys would not let us escape. (I knew they couldn't be drunk which was my original thought, because the guy was in control of his car. I figured they were on some kind of crack or something) Anyway to shorten this story up a bit, once back to town I decided to run every red light in order to attract a few cops to our plight. My friend God hung out with us for a little while longer to get us through the lights, even though He didn't feel like providing us with cops. I never did figure out why no cops, but since He does work in mysterious ways, - no matter... So we pulled into the Local Bar parking lot where my Fishing Partner works, hopped out and ran inside while the jerks in the white Bronco did a 360 or 180 (whichever is a full flip around) and drove into the parking lot where they were greeted by one of the bartenders., who sent them on their way. They were apprehended a short while later in the parking lot of a local strip club. The police most definitely were rough with them. They felt bad that two purty gals like ourselves should be able to go fishing without that sort of trauma. Man, what a night! I better check on the fish...."

After telling this story to Donna, she was compelled to confess her haircolor story and all was well. Works every time, fishing stories do. Did I go fishing that night? No. I couldn't find anyone willing to drive with me! I did however, tell that story every day for the rest of the week much to the distress of the other stylists. The next year (2001) I had no fishing stories that were quite that exciting. My most exciting stories that summer all had to do with *gangsters*.

Chapter 4

I Just Wanted To Go Fishing!!!

(WARNING: FOR THE REST OF THIS STORY YOU MUST PREPARE YOURSELF FOR LARGE AMOUNTS OF CUSSWORDS. IF YOU ARE REALLY ADVERSE TO BAD CUSSING, DO NOT READ FURTHER!)

Gangsters. How did that happen? Who are the gangsters? Where do they hang out? How do I know them? Back to August 15th, or rather the week the 15th fell in, I talked all week with the Mable's, Cindy's & Donna's at Mercury about all my new drama with my Oldest Daughter Ray-Ray. What Big Daddy thought about it etc... Grandma & Grandpa. It wasn't supposed to be like this! Who was the father? What does he look like? Where does he work? What is his mother like? (she is an ex-convict who was thrown in prison when he was 6or 7, although at the time I did not know this) What was his name? (Gabe is his name. Probably for the angel, only he didn't turn out very angelic) I should have taken her fishing! Meanwhile, Tiny sympathetically would offer words of encouragement, our

I Just Wanted To Go Fishing !!!

Manager would flair her nose, enraged that once again Ray-Ray. was sucking my energy away from the salon. Thank God Big Daddy was either away working or hunting. If he had been home, he probably would have gone to jail like all other citizen vigilantes do who mean well.

The week dragged on and on. Never ending. Hair-do after hair-do. I pondered on the conversation I had had with Gabe's mother on the phone that first day. She said he was a no good *gangbanger*. Gangbanger? What exactly did that mean? Did the word gangbanger mean that he was in a gang, or did it mean that he just wore ill-fitting pants? She said he was a worthless piece of shit. Did that just mean that he had no ambition? Was he a fisherman? More than likely not. Ray-Ray says he was nice. Caring. Excited to be a father. Possibly getting married. Hmmm I must meet this young man. Decide for myself. Maybe get to know him on the river. He was after all going to be the father of my first grandchild. Hmmm... I would wait a week or so. I couldn't take it all in at once. Plus I didn't think that I wanted to be stuck with her and him at camp. Besides she didn't want me to meet him yet. That much was obvious. I found myself entertaining thoughts of hiring her back into the salon. So what did I do? What else could I do? I went fishing!

Daizy went that time. It was raining. With the rain, there are always fish. Silvers this time - loads of them. Once again I put Daizy on a big hole full of them. I caught mine and rushed back to camp to get the kids and Chewie the dog. By the time we raced back down the river and crossed it twice, the fish had moved out of the hole. No fish for Daizy or the kids. But a Bar BQ for me with baked beans was in order. After that, while driving home, I made resolve to meet this Gabe and make plans with them. Plus Labor Day was coming the next week. The last big fishing festivity. Maybe I would invite Ray-Ray. After all, what better family time is there than fishing? None as far as I am concerned.

Also, that week on the way to blueberry picking I had to stop at Ray-Ray's house to pick up a Bloodhound puppy that she had at her house. She had "rescued" it, and I happened to see the tearful ad placed by it's true owners in the lost and found. I felt it my duty to see that it got back to it's owners. At the door I had a run-in with two lovely individuals (an Italian looking kid , and Gabe's unseen sister Jenny) who had serious gangsta accents who were unwilling to wake her up. I let them know that they did not want me coming in there, and that someone had better go get her up - which tan kid did. They all call her Ray-Ray which is how I came up with her name for the purpose of this story. Anyway, I took the dog, brought it to it's owners and returned to her house with a reward for "rescuing" the dog. One more time she got something for nothing.

I also laid eyes on the father of my grandchild's chest which looked smallish in the dark as he gestured for me to hand over the reward. I never got to see his face. I left there feeling scared and infuriated.

Finally! In two more days it would be Labor Day. There were flies to tie. Camping food to purchase. Clients to cancel (just kidding). Also, this time Camp Dad was supposed to join us. Maybe Big Daddy would come from across the bay to fish with us. I even invited Ray-Ray as a welcome back gesture (hopefully) to the family. We would leave on Friday morning.

I was feeling rather pleased that she had finally seen the light. You see, she had confessed to me that she had ruined her life, and that she had kicked Gabe out of her home. Yes, I was very pleased although a bit apprehensive. What would it be like to hang out with her again? Would it be tense? Would it be fun? Would I pretend like she wasn't pregnant with a "gangbanger's" baby? Gosh! We were just going fishing for the love! Why was I being such a weirdo? I still hadn't met this Gabe. This person who was with my daughter most of the summer. This person who took her on her only fishing trip of the season, which in itself was disgusting because they were snagging kings *while they were spawning.* Anyway.....

Friday morning came. It turned out that I would be unable to leave when I wanted because the salon was calling. I would be stuck there. I had two clients. It was cool though because one was Cindy and the other one was just a haircut. Wouldn't take long at all. I just had to call Ray-Ray and let her know. She had become a car washing girl. (A girl with her school paid for, with a career became car washer. *At least she was working.)* I dialed her number. Rrrriiiing!!!!!!! As she answered the phone I noticed that her voice sounded strange. I inquired what was wrong. She said nothing, she had been visiting with Gabe. Gabe! What's this?! I thought she had kicked him out the evening before, and stated so! Turns out that he had invited himself back in by way of the window. Did she call the cops? No of course not. Did she ask Mother to come to the rescue? Why, that would be a yes. So off I went. But first a quick call to the salon to let them know I would be saving Ray-Ray from a possible girlfriend beater or something. They would have to cancel my two clients.

It was a glorious day, lots of sunshine. A perfect day to bounce Gangsta Boy out on his head. It was also the perfect day for a drive down to the fishing hole, which you remember, was what the original plan was for the day. So much for plans - which is why I don't usually make plans. My new plan would be to meet this nice young man, kick his ass, take care of any other business there, and then go fishing. Yeah, that sounded good. Good thing I watch the World Wrestling Federation (now called World Wrestling Entertainment) every week, and had been practicing Stunners, Rock Bottoms, DDT's and such. I would need some of these moves I was sure. If only I could do some of the Hardy's high flying moves!

Cell-phone in hand, 911 punched in (in case of a confrontational mishap), I jumped out of my car and walked up to the door. Knocked twice. Two pit bulls came to the door. They seemed friendly which was good. I could see a person lying on the couch sleeping. Was that Gabe? I was certainly wishing that I knew what he looked like. Hmmm. She was taking her time to get to the door, so I opened it quietly. She was peering out of the bathroom at me, motioning for me to come to her. I looked at the sleeping boy on the couch. He was a handsome little Italian guy (the same one from blueberry day?) who reeked of cheap whisky, and was most definitely passed out. That couldn't be him. Or could it? Where was her roommate Angel? Was he passed out too? (I had met him once before with Big Daddy and liked him) What the heck was going on here? It was only the night before she said nobody was there. The stench of dogs, cats, incense and alcohol breath was overpowering. I could feel the asthma coming on. I just hoped I lasted long enough to do whatever it was that she asked me to come for.

I looked back down the hall to her, and put my hands up. Questioning. She put her finger to her lips. Shhh.. Come in here was the whisper. She looked scared and more awake than I had seen her the last time I was there (the blueberry/bloodhound time). I could feel my heart beating fast. I asked if that was Gabe on the couch. No, it was Capone. Eight questions I asked:

1. Who was Capone?
2. Where was Angel?
3. Where was Gabe?
4. Did he leave?
5. Did he hit her?
6. Why was I here?
7. What did she want me to do?
8. Why didn't she call the cops?

Lets see,

1. Capone was a "friend".
2. Angel was sleeping in his room.

3. Gabe was in her room sleeping.

4. No he didn't leave - obviously if he was in her room.

5. No, he did not hit her.

6 & 7. I was there to meet him and kick him out and make her feel brave...

8. Cops won't do anything.

So after the quick questions, and satisfied with the answers, down the rest of the hall we went. I was a tad nervous I must say. It had been quite awhile since I had ever been asked to physically help remove someone! I wasn't scared mind you, I was just nervous.   Tip toe, through the old socks, past the cat box......... (hummed in your head to the tune of Tip-Toe Through The Tulips) Just joking about the cat box. I could smell the cat box. I just couldn't see it. Anyone could have smelled it for miles I was thinking... We came to the door which was shut. I looked back at Ray-Ray, who was twiddling her fingers in the anticipation of witnessing the removal of her handsome though mean spirited boyfriend. I nodded to her. I was going in!

After swinging the door open, I was treated to the sight of a scrawny, bare back whose skin was rather yellow in color. Yuk! He must be a druggy or something I thought. He was on the bed alright and was definitely not moving. What a pig sty the room was! Clothes everywhere. An overturned box was to the right of the door. Above that suspended from the ceiling, was a macrame table thing loaded with candles. Rather gothic looking. In the right corner of her room, also suspended were two or three hairdressing mannequin heads we had decorated years ago to look like dead people for Halloween. The heads watched over the bed in a macabre sort of way. Creepy really. The smell of incense and candles was overwhelming. And cat shit! I swear she let the cats shit in her room! Anyway, back to Gabe.

I flipped on the light. "Hello! You must be Gabe! I have come over to meet you at long last. Roll over and introduce yourself." I could feel an adrenaline rush coming on. He was unmoving but I could tell that he could hear me because that scrawny back stiffened up. I couldn't wait to see his face! I wondered what he looked like. She always had the worst taste in boys. Boys not men. She was after all only 19 years old. "Gabe, get up! It's time we get acquainted."

Gabe:Why 'da fuck should I get up? Fuck you!

Me:*Because you need to meet the Grandma of your future kid you stupid fuck*!

Gabe:Fuck you whore! You a stupid whore!

Me:*Listen you fucking piece of white trash, you need to leave here. Get up and get the fuck outta here!*

That got him! He rolled over and I gazed upon the face of my future grandchild's father. And let me tell you, he was uuuugly! And mean looking! He had a big red sty that needed to be lanced on his left eye - hideeeeeeous! His eyes were bulging and blue, as well as extremely bloodshot. Bluish, purple-ish bags under his eyes. Yellowish, jaundiced skin. No doubt from the evening before. His mouth was so puckered up that it looked as if he had a cleft palate (you know, hairlip?), which would have been just fine if he did have one. He was bald except for the fag-tag on the back of his head. The letters GTS were tattooed on the right of his neck. His earring was a gun. He had other tattoo's as well, lot's of them. His chest was scrawny and hairless. He was so repulsive - I couldn't believe that she could kiss that boy, much less sleep with him. And I thought her taste was bad before! Whooooowee! He was a prize! Of course I had to mention that too.

Me:*Well Ray, I can see that your taste certainly hasn't improved! I dare say that this one takes the cake in ugly. In fact, he's the ugliest piece of shit I had ever laid eyes on in this close proximity. How disgusting! I can see why you want him out.* I went on for awhile about how white trash inbreds from the Valley were more attractive. YUK! If you have ever seen an inbred from the Valley, you will know what I am talking about.

Now the whole time I was saying my words describing my motherly disgust, he was spouting off about how he lived here, and that I was a ho, that Ray was a stupid bitch etc. He was definitely getting mad at the situation. How dare anyone come into the bedroom and disrupt his beauty sleep when in such desperate need of it!. The nerve! I didn't blame him one bit!

Then he sat up further and leaned forward towards me. He had some serious veins pulsing in his temples and his neck. He was pondering on kicking my ass and said so. Several times. He reached for the phone on the floor and began to dial out. Staring at me. Hatred vibes were bouncing off him. I asked him if he was calling the Ambulance For The Ugly, and that he really needed to get that sty fixed while he was Hospital For The Ugly. Something like that. I told him once again to get out.

So while he was dialing (and I was dialing 911 on my cell phone and mentioning to him that I was calling the cops) he was saying, "Naw, I'm callin' m'ride you fuckin' whore. Fuck you bitch. My mom's a fuckin' whore like you too. She ain't shit neither. Jus' like you. So fuck you! Call tha cops! Dey ain't movin' me neither cuz I live here foo! 'Les *you* kin move me. I tol' you, I ain't leav'n. I'll jack u'firs' fo you touch me bitch!"

That did it for me. He was going to "jack" me? I don't think so. I was calling the cops to my rescue. Cops are my friends, unless they want to give me speeding tickets! They would come and remove this psycho idiot! That was for sure. But you know what? You have to *turn on* a special 911 function on the cell phone *before* you can have an emergency! So you guessed it! It didn't work! So I did what any mother would do. I reached over and grabbed that bald headed piece of work by his bald head and scrawny arm and I flung him right off the bed! He was light as a feather. Man I was definitely having an adrenaline rush. (In my mind, I was in the wrestling ring doing a hurrican-rana off the turnbuckle on him, pinning him to the floor for my next move.) Then I sat down in the exact spot he was formerly in, stared at him like he did me, and with shaking hands dialed 911. Boy did that make him mad! Not dialing 911, it was grabbing his head that he didn't like. Plus I scratched him accidentally with my ring.

"911 Emergency. What is your emergency?"

I told her the problem as my new friend Gabe started to fling his arms around (throwing gang signs) and all sorts of cussing came from him. Boy was he mad!! Ray-Ray was very pleased with herself. Mother would make him do what she could not! The 911 lady was getting impatient with me too. I was asked to describe him which I did, While I was describing him, he started throwing some more gang signs at me (I just thought he just looked like a big ape so I did it back at him), and he was yelling, "They know me! I am Gabriel Clark-Aigner! I am with the GTS! They know me! You tell em' who I am bitch! I'm with the GTS! I *am* the GTS!!" And he stormed out through bedroom door and Ray followed him out where they were arguing loudly.

So I asked the 911 lady whether or not she could hear them and she said she could, and I asked what was taking the cops so long, and then it sounded like he hit her, and I said so. He didn't, it just sounded like it. He said he should kill her, kill the baby, kill me, wished the baby was dead, all sorts of horrible things. I told the 911 lady all this. So here he came again. Flinging more gang signs. Yelling he was going to fuck somebody up, that this was bullshit. That he lived here. And then he raised his hand to punch me, then instead he put his fist through a mirror. Blood flew everywhere! Gallon's of it!

With the mannequin heads watching me with their sightless stare, I jumped up and imitated him some more, and hollered what a big man he was, and that I had another mirror handy for him to hit if he wanted, and that he looked like a big freakin' ape. He could see that he wasn't going to get anywhere with me and so he determined to leave. Out the door he went, right into the arms of the cops who backed up quick when they saw how bloody he was! I thanked 911, hung up and followed Gabe out to the cops. Our saviors. Yay!

"Get the fuck back in the house!" were the words that came out of the first cop's mouth. He was tall with curly hair. What's this? *Get the fuck back in the house???* I figured that he must have thought I was one of the weirdos that lived there.

Me:"Sir, you need to arrest this man! He broke in and............"

Cop:"Get the fuck back in the house I said. Ma'am do what I say!"

Me:"No! You don't understand! I called you! He............"

Cop:"I said get in the house!"

So I did. *What was going on here? Why was that cop mean with me?* I'll tell you why. He thought I was White Trash Mama, come to save the day! I was confused. And where did Capone go? Was he in Angel's room? Ray-Ray's eyes looked as if they would pop out of her head. I couldn't possibly know what she was thinking at that moment. With all that I know now, *she was probably thinking, what have I done?.........* At any rate, I was going to find those boys and someone was going to give me some answers!

Me:Where are you boys at?!?!?

Ray:They're in Angel's room.

Me:You boys come out here! Now! I started down the hall.

Boys:Naw! We ain't comin out!

Me:Get out here! *If you don't come out here I'll break the fucking door down!* They probably didn't think that I could. They didn't know me very well. I could have broken down that door faster than the Tasmanian Devil!

Ray: She'll do it too! You should come out!

Boys: NO! We're naked!

Me: I don't care if you're naked! I've seen winkies before! Here I come! And I started down the hall. I knew perfectly well that they weren't naked! Dumbasses. What did they take me for? An idiot?

Boys: We're comin'. And they opened the door and came out. Fully clothed I might add.

Me: Angel! What's going on here? Why did you let Gabe in here? You live here too! You should have kicked him outta here! That's disrespecting Ray-Ray!

Angel: You shouldna done that. You shouldna touched Gabe. Ur gonna get cut!

Capone: Yup. Gonna get cut.

Me: Whatr' you talkin' about? Get cut. What's get cut? Like with a knife? You guys are afraid of him! That's what. I just tossed him out by his head! He's not shit! There are two of you!

Angel: You shouldna done that. Aw-ite? I ain't fraid o' him. I jes have respect. He's Gabe. I don' need all his boyz doin' a curb job on me.

Me: Aha! You are afraid of him! he's a scrawny little fuck. And ugly too! And what's the GTS anyway.

That question caused all three to squirm and laugh nervously. Hmmm.. What the hell was the GTS? Now for sure I wanted to know. I looked out of the window. The cops had Gabe all handcuffed and flung up across the hood of the cop car. Good! Neighbors were beginning to flock to the scene.

Capone: GTS is a car or sumthin' I think. Whatchu think Angel? Yeah, that's what it is. A car. (much nervous laughter at that one.) You shouldna touched Gabe, that's what.

Just then the cops came in. They said hello to the boys by name. They knew them by name! Hmmm.... One cop took Ray into the back to question her. The

I Just Wanted To Go Fishing !!!

curly haired one asked me who I was and how I came to be there. Finally, he was ready to listen. I wondered if I was going to get to go fishing at a decent hour today!

Me: I'm Ray's mother. I called you guys.

Cop: Yeah? So?

Me: You don't understand. I'm her mother. She called me and asked me to come over to help her get rid of him. He was yelling all sorts of stuff and threatened me and so I called you.

Cop: Yeah? And? (Arms folded. Almost glaring at me. Definitely condescending)

It came to me that these guys were used to coming over here. They thought I was White Trash Momma, come to save the day! That's what! So I mentioned that I *did not* know what was going on here. I only knew that I had disowned her for the whole summer, she got pregnant with Gangbanger Gabe's baby, and that she called me to help her! What was wrong with that? A look of surprise came over that guys face. His stern look disappeared. "Let's go outside for a minute ma'am." and so we did.

So I went on to explain the whole sordid story as far as I knew it. Including all the events of that morning. How I ended up there. How we were supposed to go fishing that afternoon. Asked what the GTS is. Asked how he knew the boys inside. Asked lots of things. Wondering. Plus I told him my name.

Cop: Let me get this straight. Your daughter is pregnant with that guys baby?

Me: Yes. And what a prize I might add.

Cop: What was he doing when he said he was with "the GTS"? Are you sure that's what he was saying? He *said* GTS?

Me: Of course that's what he was saying. How would I know those letters? What's going on here? Plus he was acting like a big ape and flinging his arms *around, and hollering that he was with the GTS, so I imitated him and made fun of him.*

Cop: The GTS is the name of his gang. He's the leader of the gang. He's a very dangerous individual. You shouldn't have made fun of him!

Me: Ha! Dangerous? I just single handed threw him off the bed! He's nothin' but a punk kid! Gang? What's that supposed to mean? Like he hangs out downtown at the transit center and harasses people? Like he deals drugs? What? He's a piece of shit!

Cop: He would just as soon shoot you as to look the other way. Let me tell you. It is not safe for your daughter here. If you can get her out of town that would be great. If she stays here............

Me: Out of town? I can send her across the bay with my husband. (Big Daddy was still working out of town and had no idea that this crap was going on) *She could stay there till the job was done.*

Cop: You're not understanding me. Do you watch television? Dateline? 20-20? Cops? That's what this is. We have been keeping an eye on her house for awhile now. *(for what?)* Pay close attention to me. Your daughter is in real danger here. If he was to show up on my property I would shoot him myself, and I'm not talking wound, I'm talking kill him. That's how dangerous I think he is. I'm personally scared to death of him. He gets off on putting his gun in people's faces. Now I don't know what your money situation is, but if you can, you need to get her out of state. And you better hope that this guy doesn't know where you live. He'll be coming to pay you a visit."

I'll tell you what! I was thinking all sorts of things right then. I was not getting what this guy was telling me. What the heck was Ray-Ray into? It was such a beautiful day. Sunshine. Such sparkly sunshine too. Blue sky. Fishing to be done. Cops. Flies to tie yet. Gangsters. Camping groceries to get. Pit bulls running around. What the hell was going on here!!! *I DON'T GET IT!!*

Cop:Now listen to me. The first thing you need to do is get an emergency restraining order against him. Get her on a plane. Don't let her come back. Ever. She needs to move. Do not tell anyone what you are doing. You are not safe here either. Don't tell anyone what you are doing OR where she is going. Sort of a witness protection. If she stays here she will probably end up dead. (Little did I know that she had already had a gun to her head for a bad drug deal)

Me:You gotta be shittin' me! Are you serious? OUT OF STATE??? I felt as if I was in the Twilite Zone. On another planet. Anywhere but Anchorage, Alaska! *Are the boys inside gangsters too???*

Cop:"We've had a couple of run-in's with the younger one Capone, but not the other one." (he said some other stuff which I don't recall because now I wasn't listening. I was thinking about What To Do) "Let's go back inside."

Back in we go. Boy did her house stink! That cat box definitely could not be disguised by the incense that was for sure! I was embarrassed and then thought - why be embarrassed? - this house wasn't mine. My inhaler came in handy that day! The boys were where we left them. The phone was ringing off the hook. In fact, it had started ringing before I ever went outside with the cop. The people on the other line wanted to know why Gabe was in the cop car! They were watching us! From where? Ray-Ray and her cop came out of her room.

The po-leece (gangster for police) readied themselves to leave with their prisoner. Their gaze upon Ray-Ray was fixed and a bit disconcerting I must say. They left after reminding me of the advice I had been given. Wowweee! What a morning. I turned to the boys. I plopped my self down next to Capone, and apologized to him for interrupting his hangover. Asked him why he was here. Told him that he was too young and handsome to be hanging out with the white trash GTS leader. Asked him where his parents were. His dad was abusive and his mom was taking care of his younger brother who was schizophrenic. We had a little chat about that sort of stuff and he gave me a hug. The whole time Ray and both boys were stealing secret knowing glances at each other. I was making a fool of myself I presumed, but I didn't care.

I also found out during that half hour that all these kids definitely didn't want to cross paths with Gabe. And I found out that Ray had a gun put to her head in her own house (bad ecstacy deal), had her dog stolen by the same guy with the gun, and then got threatening phone calls about him killing her dog. So Gabe and his boys went over to this guys house and beat him with his own guns, stole his drugs and money AND got her dog back! After returning to Rays house they all had a photo shoot marking the occasion! I have a copy of this picture. So then we left. We must go to the courthouse to get the restraining order.

I had to call the salon first and tell them a bit about what was going on. Tiny had tears for the drama of the day. I would have to get back to them later. Amazingly enough, it was still morning.

As we drove to the courthouse, Ray went on about how she *was the most educated of all the gang. Did that make her proud I wondered?* More than stupid I would say!! She became like the gangs mother. Teaching them proper manners and stuff. Did that make her proud? It sure sounded like it. She said that they were all so respectful of her. DUH! She was the leaders girlfriend! Hello! She was having his baby! They stayed at her house! The cop said that made the baby the GTS's baby! Made her the leader of the girls side. Everyone (gangsters) would be concerned about it. For the love of God! What in the heck! How gross! How disgusting! Why was I helping her! What would Big Daddy say? I told her she shouldn't have the baby. She said too bad. OK then..... Why have the cops been watching her house? Why was she with such a dangerous, disgusting person?

I was after all her mother. Hmmm.. What were my obligations here? I guess I would do pretty much anything for my kids. Even one who was a gangster. I still was in a bit of a shock. The restraining order was a breeze. I filled out most of it. Of course I made the mistake of putting my address on it. Little did I know that Gabe would receive an exact copy of it. Remember? It was important that he not know where I lived! Damn it!

That afternoon, back at her house, the boys were long gone. There were bags to pack, cats to feed and dogs to take. There were actually three pitbulls there. Cobain, Doja and Mystery Puppy. The phone rang non-stop. Gangster girls were coming by to give Ray-Ray messages from Gabe. What a stench there! Whew! There was even a couple of dog turds on the floor next to pizza crust! Anyway, one phone call suggested that we get out quick. The house was to be shot up. (that's why there were no boys there - they had already received the warning) Someone was going to busta few caps on us. Retaliation I suppose. The cats would have to stay there for a couple of days. We would bring the dogs though. Three freakin' pit bulls. Big Daddy was going to love this one when he found out! So after what seemed eternity, we left. Driving off we could hear the "hoodrats" (scummy gangster girls) yelling that we better leave Cobain - he belonged to Gabe.. Keeping that dog for her was the beginning of the next drama! I couldn't wait till she got on that plane! *I JUST WANTED TO GO FISHING!!!!!* Shit.

The next day after "cold-lampin in the crib" (hanging out at home) together, it was time to put her on the plane. I needed to get her there before she changed her mind. Yes, I would take care of the dogs, cats, sell her house, send her "jonx" (worldly belongings) to her. I was her mom. Of course I would. Plus I wanted to run away from her. What do I tell the kids? What do I tell everyone else? What was I going to do with three pitbulls and two cats? Good grief! Shit, I still had to pack for camping. If I was still going to go.

While driving back to the house, I determined that I would get rid of the dogs, except maybe Doja, and that would be that. Maybe this Gabe could find Cobain in the pound. But then again, if he found him in the pound, then She would find out & be mad at me. Stupid, yes. But at the time I thought it. I realized that I was actually afraid of her, afraid of my own daughter. I started to look forward to finally leaving for my shortened fishing extravaganza..

Once home I got out of the car. What was that sound assaulting my ears? The dogs! I could hear a massive dog fight going on in the back of the house! I raced out the back door. The kids were screaming, holding on to their beautiful Chooey dog (she is a lovely Bull Mastiff who snorts, drools, farts loud powerful farts, and is a giant love machine) What the.... Cobain (formerly used in dog fighting) grabbed the youngest pup and threw him off the deck, dived down the stairs and proceeded to rip the pups tummy open. Blood everywhere. Kids yelling. Puppy wailing. Me yelling at them to get Chooey and Doja outta there. He was killing that puppy! I grabbed a shovel and bashed him in the head twice and screamed in my best gangster voice, *COBAIN!* He dropped that puppy once and went for him again, so I bashed him in the head again. I thought now I am for sure going to get it. I yelled *COBAIN!* again and he stopped, looked at me and was all done. I muzzled him up with a leash and we tossed him in a kennel. The puppy was still bawling and so I grabbed him up and held him close. I expected his insides to fall out, but just his tummy skin was torn. Thanks to God. Plus the poor little thing had crapped on himself, so now I was wearing blood, dog fur and puppy crap. I ace bandaged him up and called Pet Emergency. The pound came and took Cobain, and we finally went fishing I do not know if the puppy lived, or what became of Cobain. We did however catch lots of fish. Although it wasn't as fun because of the hideous turn of events.

I didn't even have fun searching for fish on the Russian which is always a blast. My Fishing Partner was rather perplexed with me. I had no explanation for him. For one thing, he has this idea (which is true and legit) that I shouldn't let things that I have no control over bother me. I had told him the story and he was like "AND?". You know, *and why are you letting something bother you that you can't change?* He also gave the words of wisdom that I always dramatize everything out of proportion (which is quite possibly true) and that I was being a girl again (meaning I was getting too emotional about something I couldn't change). Anyway, that day I was all done fishing and said so. To this day he doesn't get that whole thing. Neither do I. All I know is that for the first time in my life I didn't feel like fishing - which sucked. Big time.

Chapter 5

Cats, Guns, & Inbreds!

That Tuesday I went off to work. Boy did I have a story for all the clients! Wooowie! The stylists would tire of this one soon that was for certain! Tiny would offer tears of sympathy, Hoochie would flare her nose in justified anger at Ray-Ray (who in her opinion was no good anyway) and Lil' Dancer would politely listen and then apologize for eavesdropping. It would be this way from here on out. Always the same. When I got off work that night I would take a police escort over to her house to get the cats. I wondered if Gabe had been released from jail yet.

    I decided to call Ray-Ray right away. Have you talked to any of your gangster friends? How did you get into this mess? Is Angel a GTS gangster? What do the rest of them look like? Do they know where I work? Do any of them know where I live? Did she think the girls from next door would bother me? What was Angelo's number? (She had told me that he wanted to get in to get his stuff). I told her that I would be taking the cops and Angel could come.

After hanging up with her, I promptly called Angel. Yes he would like to come, and no we don't need cops. Why not I asked? He said that I would be safe with him and that he thought Gabe was still in jail. The real reason he didn't want the cops there was because he didn't want the gang to think that he was working with the cops. Fine then. I would pick him up at 7:00pm. I figured that I should bring my own protection, so I left the house with a strapped on .44 mag & a .22 semi-auto underneath my coat. Let me tell you, I don't even know what I was thinking when I did that, it just sounded like a good idea. Plus I was a tad bit sceeeered.

Angel is a handsome, hip-hop looking guy with an easy smile. I make him nervous because he says my eyes bore into his head. Anyway, he was happy that we were going cop-less, although he did confess that he too was nervous. Not scared mind you, just nervous. Of course you know I drilled him on the GTS and whether he was a gangster or not, and if not how is it that he gets along with them so well... He answered all my questions.

Angel: Naw, I jus' kick it withem now and then. Smoke a little gank an' jus' hang out. You know. They come over to the crib an' I jus' be cool withem. Naw, I don' even like Gabe. I jus' gotta be cool withim'. (He would talk gangstery and try not to at the same time. It was funny listening to him try not to sound like he wasn't street talking)

We came to the top of her street. Adrenaline rushes were going to become a common thing I was pretty sure. In fact, by the end of September, I forgot what it felt like to not have the adrenaline. By the end of that month, I actually *craved* some kind of dangerous encounter so that I wouldn't be so tired. Talk about tired! Oh! Where was I? At the top of her street... (that's what I do. I ramble. It drives some people crazy) There were children running about, families having bar-bque's, you know, people who are oblivious to any danger lurking in the neighborhood.

As we sat there at the top of the street waiting for the right moment to drive in, it occurred to Angel that there truly might be some gangster repercussions if we were caught going into the house. Maybe Gabe was already there. Maybe there were others. Maybe they would come shoot us while we were in there. One thing was for sure. We weren't going to know anything by just sitting there. So we started down. Have you ever heard of the band Limp Bizkit? They have a song that says "Keep rollin'rollin'rollin' rollin on. Keep rollin' rollin' rollin' rollin......." I like that song. It started playing in my head after my next question was answered.

Me: So what are we gonna do if he is there?

Angel: We're jus' gonna roll on by. Jus' keep on rollin'

Keep rollin' rollin' rollin' on............ And so we rolled on into her drive. I was thinking of chickening out, but since I had taken up gun-slinging.... *Keep rollin' rollin' rollin' - I'm gonna kick her ass.....* I opened the door. I forgot to breathe which was a good thing cause the cat stench was extra potent that day - what with the house being closed up and everything. All was quiet except for the meowing of the cats which were quickly stuffed into a kennel. There seemed to be extra trash everywhere, but I wasn't sure. Angel started down the hall.

BAM! BAM! BAM! was the sound of the knocking! Shit! *Angel! Get over here! What should we do? Answer the door?* BAM! BAM! BAM! "Open the fuckin' door!" And so I did.

I opened the door to the inbred, green toothed, gangster girl from next door with the gun pointed straight to her forehead. She didn't flinch although her eyes widened with surprise. She was uglier than Gabe. Well, almost. "I wanna talk to Ray." she said. I told her that she wasn't there. She said she was coming in to see for herself. So, being the gracious hostess that I am, I invited her in to have her brains blown out. She declined and gave me a message. It was that Gabe wanted his dog back and that he was coming to my house, that he knew where I lived and that he was going to "cap" me. I thanked her for the message and shut the door on her. I just knew that we were going to be in the middle of a big shoot out. *"Hurry up Angel!"*

Angel started down the hall but got sidetracked. He spied a couple of large bongs on the counter top and thought it would be appropriate to take a couple of hits. But first he must scrape some resin out. I let him amuse himself for a couple of minutes while I gathered up the cat-food, bowls and other pet supplies. *Hurry up Angel or you lose your stuff!* Finally, he finished and we carried everything out of the house. The beauty queens from next door were watching us with cell phones in hand. My daughter is such a fool I was thinking. How could she hang out with this filthy scum? These people with green teeth. These people who have no regard for anything decent. *How are you gonna stay out of trouble with the gang I asked. They are going to want to know why you are with me, right?* I felt sick to my stomach. I was getting nervous. The longer we stayed here....... What had Ray-Ray gotten me into?

He said that he would clear everything up. So while I was checking her mail, he went into their house to "bum a smoke". He explained to them that I was shopping at the store that he worked at, and that I offered him to take him with me to get his stuff. he accepted and that was how he came to be with me. That was quick thinking. I was ready to start rollin' on. And so we did. After unloading at his parents house, he gave me a hug and I went home with my new cats. Gangster kitties. A yellow one named Jerry (we gave it to her as a kitten) and a turtle shell called Sasha (we went with her to pick that one out). They meowed all the way home and when we got there, they proceeded to beat up my own cat, scratch up my furniture and give me one of many asthma attacks that afflicted me for the rest of the year.

I made a decision that night after talking with Daizy. (I had informed her that I was going into Gangsterville with a possible gangster and that if she didn't hear from me by 8:00 to call the cops.) My decision was that I would research this gang. The GTS. See what I was up against. See if they were *really* a threat. See what Ray-Ray had gotten herself into. Just see...........

The first logical choice of phone calls would be to the police station I figured. The dispatcher told me to call the prosecutors office, who gave me a different phone number, who gave me a cop shop phone number who gave me another number of a person in town who specializes in the local gang scene, At last! Someone who could tell me the deal. I left a message on his recorder to call me back anytime. ASAP! I would go to coffee with this person and learn about the GTS. We would have a nice chat and he would fill me in. I wondered what the letters GTS stood for. I wondered what it meant to be the leader's girlfriend. I wondered if all the punk kids in the gang were drug dealers or petty thieves. I wondered how dangerous they all really were.........

Wonder, I did! For the next two days. You know when you think you are being blown off? Avoided? That's what I thought. Maybe there *was* no GTS. Maybe the cop that arrested Gabe was just paranoid. Maybe I sent Ray-Ray off for no reason. Let me tell you! MAYBE was going to drive me crazy! Either "maybe" would, or the goings on at the salon would.

Finally, the call I had been waiting for came at 9:30 that Wednesday night. It was Officer Ryan. He would answer my questions about the GTS.. In fact, he said that he was interested in how much influence I had on Ray-Ray, and that my name had come up in a meeting of cops that day. (odd don't ya think?) he wanted to know if I could meet him in the morning. Tell me where! I'll cancel my day! He would call me at the salon and we would set up a time. I couldn't wait. I called Big Daddy across the bay where he was putting the final touches on that rich guy's cabin. I told him I was going to coffee with a gang cop to find out the scoop. I could hardly wait. Plus he said that he could arrange a police escort to go get the rest of the things that I wanted to get out of her house.

I called a couple of people to tell them my news. One of them is a hairstylist friend Eva from the salon where Ray-Ray went to work after I fired her. She loves a good story as much as I do, so I figured that she would like this one. Which she did. She mentioned that a couple of years back that she heard of some people whose home was bombed by gangsters because they were working with the cops and so now she was worried about me. What did I have to go and tell her for anyway? Plus one of her clients worked for the FBI and was a girl-gang specialist. Hmmm. Now that was cool I reckoned. Too bad she wasn't a boy-gang person.

Chapter 6

Chillin' Wit' Da' Feds!

September 7, 2001 was a partly sunny/partly cloudy sort of day. No rain. I woke up anticipating what the cop would tell me. I could hardly wait to talk to him. Maybe we would have coffee at Barnes & Noble. I would bring a notebook. I would find out everything there was to know about the GTS. Hopefully I would find out why Ray-Ray joined. Just as I was walking out the door to go to the salon, the phone rang.

"Hey Mary? Listen, it's me Eva. I went and stuck my nose in your business." That wasn't surprising. She was alot like me. "I just got off the phone with my client so-and-so from the FBI, and she said under no circumstances should you bring the cops into this. She also said that she knows who is handling the case and that she was going to call him. She said that if you bring the cops over to the house you will be further 'marked' and that your name came up." Marked? What was marked? *And why did my name keep coming up in cop meetings?* I didn't do anything. I told Eva to MYOB and that she shouldn't worry and that YES I was bringing cops over and that YES I was meeting with Officer Ryan! And goodbye! And so I hung up and went to the salon.

I pondered on what Eva said as I walked up the stairs. She just had to wreck my happy mood! Quickly I flipped on the lights, made the coffee, counted the money, turned on the music, and ran the reports. I took $20.00 from the drawer for coffee with the cop and waited for the phone to ring. What if he didn't call? What if I never found out about the gangsters? Did I really need to know? Were they just a big joke? This was stupid. It was all a bad dream. Hmmmm.. Who were my clients for the day? One good thing - I didn't have anyone until 11:30am., so I had an hour and a half to talk with Officer Ryan. I was jolted out of my reverie by the phone ringing. "Good morning, Mercury Studio!"

"Hi. Mary? It's Officer Ryan. How are you?" said the person on the phone. I told him that I was fine and that I was ready for a visit. "Well then, how about you meet me at my office at 10:00." Like I knew where his office was.

I asked him if it was on Bragaw Street since that was the only place that I knew had cop offices. They probably have offices everywhere and I just don't know about them. I prepared myself to lose my parking spot.

"No. It's right down the street from your salon." (How did he know where my salon was?) "You know, the FBI Building."

"You gotta be shitting me! The freakin FBI? What has she done?" *What kind of gang research does the FBI do on punk kid gangbangers?*

"Listen Mary. It is very imperative that you don't tell a soul where you are going. It is not safe for you to let ANYONE know. Alright? I'll see you in ten minutes." Click.

What the fuck....... Holy shit. Holy bejeeeezus. The FB-freakin-I????? I couldn't believe it. What kind of gangsters were these kids? What had Ray-Ray been up to? In walked Tiny. She was looking cute that day. She opened her mouth to tell me of her Boy Stalking activities of the night before, but then stopped. She could tell something was up. "Tiny! I have to go now. Remember that I called all those phone numbers to find out about gangs?" She said yes. "Well I'm not supposed to tell anyone, but I have to go to the FBI. Can you believe it? What do ya think she has done? Don't tell anyone where I am going. I wasn't supposed to tell you. Now I have. I am probably going to get arrested for telling you. SO don't tell anyone. Big Daddy is going to love this one! I'm going to kick Ray's ass when I see her again!"

So I gathered my things and walked out. I had colored my hair black so as to be incognito, and I wondered if anyone would recognize me. I put on my sunglasses and walked down the street. Past the State Trooper Museum, past the wolf gift store, across C Street, down past the empty lot/park area, and bumped into Lil' Dancer. She had a bright sunny smile for me and wondered where I was going. I said for a stroll. She knew I was lying but was ok with it.

The FBI building is rather an imposing place. You can't see in. The windows are tinted and look mirror-like when you gaze upon them. There are cameras watching you amidst the decorative bushes. I felt the urge to breath my asthma inhaler several times before summoning up the courage to go in. At that moment for the first time in my life, I wished that I looked like somebody's "mother" rather than a crazy hairdresser. I wanted to look respectable. Not someone who this fellow would look at like a stupid, unintelligent, old lady-wannabe-cool fool. Of course while I was pondering these things and puffing away on my inhaler, the front desk security was calmly watching me from the inside. Probably making fun of me as I am sure they do every other person who stand outside of those doors wishing they looked more distinguished. I walked in.

Wow! What a sight! Panels of television screens lined the walls. Walk-

I Just Wanted To Go Fishing !!!

through security like the airport. Computer stuff, cameras and two dorky looking security guards. These guys were probably either rent-a-cops or secret black belt karate guys made to look dorky. Anyway, all this stuff made me nervous. They showed to the elevators where I would ride up to the office and check in with the receptionist.

The receptionist was a stuffy puckered up old bat who assured me that Officer Ryan would be right out. I wondered what he would look like. The waiting area was rather sparse. It definitely needed some different reading material. No People Magazine there. A giant picture of President Bush adorned the wall. A flag. The FBI mission statement to serve and protect.... Cameras. Shit. I just knew that guy was watching me to see if I was nervous. Maybe even a whole panel of guys. I did my best not to look nervous. I didn't do anything! I was here for personal research! And then, what was I doing there? At that moment I couldn't remember. Then I heard a door open. A lady walked out.

She was athletic looking. Brown hair. I was betting she could kick some ass. "Mary. I'm Lucy. Officer Ryan will be right out." Unsmiling, she shook my hand. Lucy was my friend Eva's hair client! Hmmm. Why did I have the feeling that I was in trouble? Freakin' Eva anyway! I told her that I had spoken with Eva that very morning and that her name had come up. She figured that it did. Just then a tall man came out. It was Officer Ryan.

As I gazed upon the face of him it occurred to me that he didn't look like what I pictured an FBI guy to look like. He looked like a fun baseball player type who liked the outdoors. Plus he smiled alot. Definitely not an ass kickin' gun slingin' cop. Hmmm. I figured that Lucy here looked meaner than him. He shook my hand with a bone crusher, and they both led me to a room.

Hmmm. Just like TV. A long table with a phone. Cameras in every corner and two doors. Chairs. I sat at one of them and they sat at two others. Lucy was pretty casual and she looked kinda mean. I would not want to mess with her that was for sure. She mentioned that I should not go trying to take matters into my own hands or bring cops over to Rays house. They wanted to know all sorts of stuff:

1. How much influence I had on Ray-Ray.
2. If Ray-Ray trusted me.
3. Why I needed to get into her house.
4. What I was doing there on this date, and that date, and this date, and that date......
5. How was it that I had authority to give them permission to search her house.
6. Why I had called them.

I answered as best as I could. They had advised me to just tell the story from the beginning. All the way back to when she moved up here. So I did. I told them about hiring and firing her. I told them about all the freaks at her house. About how I figured that Ray-Ray trusted me because she was out of state now. How I wanted to get some more things from her house including pictures of me and the kids. All the dates I was there. How I had Power of Attorney to sell her house and had the keys and that was how I could give permission for a search. (Here! Take the keys!)

I told them about the day that Gabe was arrested and how I had heard that he knew where I lived. How he was flinging his arms around and yelling GTS at me. (Let me tell you, that lady was good! She explained to me about gang signs and she did the same thing and talked at the same time and explained what her crazy gestures meant! I loved it! She was awesome! Officer Ryan agreed with me about how good she was. I was mesmerized. That lady would dress up as a gangster girl and become one to bust them.)

I Just Wanted To Go Fishing !!!

I told them that Ray-Ray was pregnant with his kid. That statement brought looks of shock and disgust and what looked like worry. Hmmm...

I told about how I was scared that he was coming to my house. How I was scared that he was really going to kill me like he said. How I was scared for my kids.

It occurred to me to ask what Ray-Ray had done. Why they wanted to search her house. Why had they been watching her house. (I knew that they had because they knew all the dates I had been there) Officer Ryan said that they were unable to tell me IF she was being investigated but if she were, it would be for weapons violations, drugs & robberies. Whooooweee!! I raised a regular criminal! At the very least, a criminal lover!!! Not just a passive criminal either. A violent bunch of freaks! What happened?

They said they would try to protect my family, but that they couldn't be with me 24/7.... Hmmm.. This was frightening news indeed. Where was Big Daddy they wanted to know. (They were pleased that he was away because sometimes irate husbands and fathers foul up investigations by trying to help) They would get me into the house with them, they just had to figure out the safest way. You gotta be shitting me!

I was to go back to the salon. Get some boxes and then go home and wait for their call at 1:30. Once again I was told not to tell anyone. (Of course I told Tiny. I can't keep my big mouth shut! Plus I would have to cancel my hairdo's for the day for some sort of reason) When the phone call came I about jumped outta my shoes! "We will meet you at the school in the back parking lot." They also wondered if I would be in the green bronco. Green Bronco! Those guys are good! They know everything. So off I went.

It was sunny that afternoon. The clouds of the morning had gone. I wondered if it was sunny where Big Daddy was working. He was hard to get ahold of so he still didn't know the deal. I drove so fast to get to the school that I was there too early. Since I didn't want to look like a dork I left to get a soda and some curly fries from the Arby's up the street. I suppose they were yummy but I can't remember. I ate them behind the school in my car while I was waiting for the FBI cops. When I am waiting for people to show up, I have too much time to imagine all sorts of crazy things. This day was no different. I imagined we would find a big stash of guns. Maybe a drug laboratory of some sort. Stolen property. Who knew? Maybe a dead body under the house. Maybe some gangsters were sleeping there..... Thinking, thinking, thinking.... And then they came.

Officer Ryan was driving a green SUV of some kind. I didn't pay attention to what. His passenger wasn't the lady from the morning. It was a man who looked like one of those crazy cops from the movies. He had longish hair and a crazy look to his eyes. I knew that if anyone messed with him that they were in serious trouble! That was for sure. We were introduced but I for sure can't remember his name. I had become mesmerized by the situation. I could actually feel myself *trying* to pay attention. Officer Ryan was explaining what was going to happen:

As we were speaking, a car was driving through the cul-de-sac to see if they could see anyone in there, or any broken windows. The car would then park at the top of the street. Another car would be going down there to park. When the first car gave the go-ahead we would drive down there, me first into the driveway followed by them. The story was that they were two of my friends that were going to help me get a few things out of the house. If any gangsters came out of the house next door, I was not to raise my voice under any circumstances (they must have known that I have a bit of a temper). Also, I was not to be afraid because they would protect me (probably with all the guns that were strapped to their bodies). Also if any gangsters were to pull a gun on us that there were more guns aimed at them..... *HOLY M-F'n SHIT!!* is all I could think. Also the ATF was on standby.

Now my mind was in overdrive! The freakin ATF? Did that mean that a bunch of guys dressed in black would be hiding in the woods behind the house? Or did that mean that the ATF would drop out of helicopters or something? Talk about being on an alien planet or warp zone or something! I'll tell you what! I couldn't wait to see what would happen next. Maybe a big shoot-out and all the gangsters would get arrested in front of my very eyes! Maybe I would be the only one to get shot.... Maybe... Oh. What was he saying? Just the reminder to try and act normal. What was normal anymore????? And off we went.

I felt like I was going to pee on myself as I drove down the road. I tried not to look around for the rest of the cops like the fool that I am at times. I wore my G-Loomis hat for the occasion in case I looked nervous. Why that made me less nervous I do not know. I just know that I wore it. Where were the rest of the cops I wondered... I also wondered if there really were more cops. I wondered lots of things on that long two block drive. Her house came into view. I didn't see any gangsters. That was good. We both parked, got out of our cars, got our boxes and started walking to the door. I could see the nasty bitches (gangster gurlz) watching out of the window next door.

We got to the porch. Here they came! Green Tooth & Vee (I don't know her real name, I just know they call her Vee). They both shoved past the cops trying to act all tough and stuff. "Hey! Yo! Can I help you with sumthin'?" Greeny asked. I looked at Officer Ryan who gave me a slight nod and big stare, both of which meant to answer her but be cool about it. So I said her name and told her that I was picking up some of Ray-Ray's things. She wanted to know who the guys were. I told her that they were my friends come to help as if it was any of her business.

Then Vee pushed forward and got in my face about how some of her CD's were in there and that she wanted them back. I told her that I would be more than happy to get anything that belonged to her, but that she was NOT coming in the house that day. They both left pissed off and immediately got out their cell phones to call some crew friends. "Looks like we are gonna have company" said Officer Ryan. And in we went.

WOW! Talk about rotten cat box smell! Man! I could see that the cops noticed it right away too. I was assured by them that all gangsters like to have pets of some sort. Usually pit bulls. We set down our box's. All sorts of activity was happening now. They were all business. Out of their boxes came cameras, finger print kits, walkie talkies, a small twirling camera on a tripod, and this thing that looked like the cover of a car stereo. What cool stuff! I watched everything. Everything! So deluxe!

Officer Ryan took pictures of the whole house while the other guy held the car stereo thing over the walls. (hmmmm) Then that guy disappeared under the house with rubber gloves and some other stuff. Rubber gloves? Was he going to find bodies? Was he going to find the gun stash? Drug lab? What? What? Whaaaat?

I couldn't quit watching what they were doing. I forgot why I wanted to go there in the first place. I forgot about the pictures on the walls and fridge. Plus I could hear really, really good that day. I could hear everything. I marveled at that. I was there with the FB-freakin'-I! Can you believe it? This was craaaazy! Just then *crackle, crackle,* went the walkie talkie next to the twirling camera on the tripod. "Such & such kind of car is coming down the street. Comin' real fast. Slowing down in front of the house. He's looking in...."

Officer Ryan: License plate!?

Speaker: Number blablablabla...

Officer Ryan: Follow it!

Now wait a minute I was thinking. *"Hey that was our back-up, right?!?!?"*

This was definitely messed up. I was not into our backup guy leaving us stranded. *"Oh my God. Oh my God. Oh my God."* I kept hearing that. Who was saying that? It was me! I was the one whispering oh my God. Alot.

Officer Ryan: "Mary. Why don't you look in this bucket for anything interesting. Like cell phone bills & stuff."

That was cool. Now I had a job to do. I became focused. I searched through that bucket and had fun doing it I tell ya. I found cell phone bills, phone numbers. All kinds of useful stuff. I couldn't believe that Ray-Ray was *into* such freaks. What was she thinking? "Crackle, crackle. Here comes another car. Two individuals. Coming very fast. Slowing in front. Stopping and looking in." *SHIT!*

Officer Ryan: License plate!?

Speaker: Blablabla....

Officer Ryan: Follow it!

Now this was too much! Not only did our first car leave us but now our second car was leaving too? I couldn't take it so I jumped up and ran over to the window. I just *had* to see who was watching us! *Oh my God. Oh my God. Oh my God.....*

Officer Ryan: Mary! Come away from the window. We have more cars. Don't you worry now. We are fine. We are watching them watching us. OK? If they have a gun on us, you know we have guns on them!

I just knew for sure now that there were cops all over those woods! KNEW IT! A couple of them anyway. Plus I could almost hear the helicopters my brain had conjured... One more car came and went. But I was fine by then. I was busy with my searching chores and by then I had remembered the stuff I wanted to get. I didn't even smell the cat box anymore! Which was good. I watched as Officer Ryan collected drug paraphernalia, bullets, pieces of paper etc. The phone kept ringing too. I was not to answer it although I wanted to. Wanted to badly! I wondered what the guy under the house had found. It was becoming apparent that we weren't going to find anything very interesting up where we were. Finally he came up and I gathered that we were done. That guy had discovered that they had used the underneath of her house as a makeshift target practice range. There were bullet holes through the foundation and the daylight shone through. What idiots!!! Ooooh, Big Daddy was gonna love this!

As we prepared to leave, I was told once again not to raise my voice. I was to take my boxes of stuff out followed by one guy, and then they would both follow me out. The boxes that they brought would not be able to "fit" in my car, so they would be nice guys and offer to bring it in their car. Then I was to "remember" to look for something in her truck. Anything. The only thing I could think of would be a fishing pole since I am a dork.

With the inbreds watching out the windows and on their deck, we looked for my fishing pole. I pretended to try and start the truck while the crazy TV looking guy scooped stuff out from under the seat. We were done.

Officer Ryan: We'll just meet you at your house. (Loud enough for the inbred hoodrats or anyone else to hear.)

So off we went without too much incident. No shootouts. No SWAT Team. No ATF guys swooping out of helicopters. None of the wild imaginings I had made up! I felt relieved and a bit disappointed I must confess. Now that would have been a good story. Maybe it still was.

They pulled over back up at the school. I was right behind them. Officer Ryan got out and walked back. I looked at my watch. It was 4:15! We had been there over 2 hours!

Me: *Now what? I mean, that was a bit disappointing wasn't it? No guns found or anything........*

Officer Ryan: No, we found interesting stuff. I was hoping to find other things but this is a start.

Me: We have been here two hours! What about my kids! I have to get home! (Here came the tears! I controlled them pretty well though.)

Officer Ryan: Your kids are safe at home. Your little redhead made it home awhile ago. He smiled a fatherly smile at me. I mean, it *looked* fatherly. (Someone had followed my kids home from school. Someone to make sure that no gangsters followed them home. ((Unbeknownst to me, Gabe had gotten out of jail that afternoon. Probably he was one of the people in the cars that drove by Ray-Rays house while we were in it.))

Me: What?!?!?!?! What about tomorrow? What about the next day? I was stunned. I couldn't breathe. Not because of asthma, my lungs just forgot how to inhale. *Why were they followed home today? Hey, and how disappointing! We didn't even find any good stuff did we?!*

Officer Ryan: Just a precaution. Listen. We can't be with you all the time. You need to start paying close attention to your surroundings. And don't worry about what we found or didn't find. We got enough to get started on. All those phone numbers will be helpful. What I really want to see are the pictures that Ray-Ray is sending you. (I had told him about some pictures that she was sending me of the gang. One in particular that he was interested in) Anyway, listen. There is a woman parked behind you. She will follow you out. I want you to turn right, then left (and a whole bunch of other turns) and when it's clear, she will go around you and wave you on. You need to start doing this when you are driving. Watch in your rearview to see if you are being followed."

Wow! These guys are good! The lady behind me looked like a hockey mom who needed her hair done - maybe I should have given her a card. She was driving a white Suburban with a bunch of blankets or laundry. (She was the surveillance person who was watching the twirling camera we had with us - the blankets were covering the equipment) I wondered where she had been parked. I never even saw that car. Then he pointed to the car in front of him and said the person in it would follow him out. Can you believe it??? There must have been bunches of them watching over us! Most excellent!

I was just to go home and if anything unusual happened to call him. What was unusual anyway?? This whole thing could be called unusual couldn't it? *Call him if anything unusual...* He had given me his card earlier in the day. Call if I started getting lots of hang-up phone calls. Or when I got the pictures. So off I went, blubbering and bawling the whole way. And sure enough, the lady in the Suburban followed me and later waved me on.........

I figured that since I was really having a good cry, it wouldn't be proper to go home. So I went over to my Fishing Partner's house to continue my blubber fest. I filled him in on how I figured that know one would notice if I came up missing, and how no one would know how to get ahold of Big Daddy if someone did notice. Stuff like that. My Fishing Partner sat on his couch across the room wishing he could shut me up because I was quite out of control. Poor guy. Now he teases me out of the blue sometimes with comments like "No one will even miss me!", which is extra funny now and embarrassing! Anyway, after I was all done with the story and was certain that he would for sure notice that I was missing, I hopped in my car and pondered.....

Just wait till I get my hands on that Ray-Ray! I was about to turn into a Vigilante Gangster Killer! If I didn't kick somebody's ass then it was certain that Big Daddy would. Big Daddy!? What was he going to say about this day? Whooowee! Man! Maybe I would just go fishing and avoid the whole thing. Hmm.. There were after all, some silvers still hanging around! In the end, we just stayed home and waited for Big Ole' Ass Kickin' Daddy to come home! Home to throw some whup-ass on Gangsterville! Check out the inbreds! I resigned myself to the obvious fact that the fishing season was over for me.

Chapter 7

Yo! Big Daddy!

Big Daddy came home that weekend to get ready for hunting. He was going to cancel his hunting trip after listening to The Story, but I put a stop to that. He would just cause problems.. He wanted to pay a visit to Gabe, and maybe pummel him. Plus, we needed the moose meat. However, I still wanted to take him over to Ray-Rays house before he left and tell him The Story again. Only this time with visuals. Plus I wanted him to help me make a plan for when to get movers over there and stuff. The cops did after all say to get her out of state that first day. The day I was just supposed to go fishing. So off we went.

Now big Daddy is a calm man. He is after all a Leo. And being in the construction business running adult day care, he had been able to build up a tolerance for stupidity. Except when it came to his own kid. You know? So as we drove over there on September 9, the only words out of his mouth (there were lots of them mind you) began with phrases like "For stupid!" or "What the fuck?"... Stuff like that. His normal Minnesota monotone actually had a new ring to it. The veins were popping in his temples and his nose was rather flared. He certainly didn't look like calm, laid back Big Daddy that day. He looked like the wrestler Big Papa Pump!

I had anticipated the occasion and had bought face masks so maybe I could breathe better there. You know, with the cat box and all. As we drove up to the house, I noticed right away that the gurlz weren't watching us. *Odd.*

As I unlocked the door, I had the creepy sensation that someone was there. *In there.* No one was - a person would have to have powerful lungs to withstand the catbox stench this day! Even Big Daddy coughed and commented on it. He started down the hall towards her room where he would venture under the house. Tip toe, through the waste dump, past the cat box...

"WAIT!!!" I shouted. "Someone has been here!" I could feel it. It seemed messier in there. I pushed past Big Daddy. My heart was in my throat. The hall closet was open. That was new! I looked in Angel's room. Aha! The window had been broken with a log. Big Daddy opened her bedroom door. Clothes were everywhere. Her television was missing. Drawers dumped out everywhere. I looked at the mannequin heads staring at nothing. I wondered aloud what they had seen.... Her obnoxious collection of candles even seemed to have a story to tell. We backed out of there and went into the living room where she kept her stereo and a large collection compact discs. All gone.

As we waited for the cops to arrive, I decided to go next door and talk to her neighbor. Not the inbreds. The Other Side. The Other Side neighbor lady had called the cops on Ray-Ray severaltimes and I felt the need to apologize to her. Their two homes were attached to each other. She was a frumpy sort of woman with matronly brown hair. I figured that she had definitely been through the wringer living in Gangsterville against her will. Plus she had a little girl.

After she answered the door and got over her shock that I was actually apologizing, she told me some stories. She told me how the gang would discipline the dogs by stepping on their heads. Told me about the day a rival gang drove up, how guns were drawn, how Ray-Ray was screaming at everyone, and how the S.W.A.T. team showed up. How one day cops came because a girl had passed out on the cigarette-strewn lawn. How loud gang parties went all night long. How she feared for her little girls life - not to mention her own. I told here that she wasn't safe there and that she should leave for awhile, and she told me that she already had left for two weeks the day the S.W.A.T. team came. She told me that she had moved to Alaska to get away from all that stuff and live a nice quite life. How hideous. I felt really bad for her and her little girl and I said so.

After what seemed an eternity, a policeman finally showed up. We had aired out the house as best we could so he could breathe while doing his investigation. He took fingerprints and took some pictures. After he left, Big Daddy boarded up the window as he wiped away some tears. What had happened to his little girl? The girl he had adopted as his own? What had he done wrong?

I decided to lay a booby trap for any other intruders. I took the floor board to her basement complete with previously incrusted cat crap, and strategically placed it under the windows. Ha! *Whomever came in would leave with a remembrance!* Then we left, taking with us his old truck that he had given to her. The truck that she had never changed the title on. The truck she didn't take care of. The truck possibly used in robberies and other wrong doings. We were followed by someone over to the garage where the truck would be parked. That was ok though, because we weren't followed home.

I felt bad for Big Daddy. He must have wanted to really pummel someone. He wasn't used to the feeling of not being in charge of his life. Being told that he needed to be away from the action protecting his family was probably more than a

Mary Oyster

most men could take. I never really thought much about what he was thinking. I was too busy with my own fear and anger.

Anyway, since Big Daddy isn't much of a lover of fishing, he did what he does best. He went hunting! Good for him. Yummy for us.

Chapter 8

Movers, Treasure & Stuff

Everyone knows what happened nationally on September 11, 2001. What a horrible day. Our salon was closed that day as were most businesses located downtown. We all knew people in New York and all of us were worried. None of us wanted to work that day. Most clients were pretty understanding, all except for one man. He insisted that since the city had lifted the evacuation of downtown, we remain open so that he could get his son's hair cut that day. He had school pictures the next day! Can you believe it? We were in a national crisis and he was worried about his stupid kids hair! I was like, fuck that! I don't give a fuck if I ever see you or your kid again! You know?! Plus I had my own local terrorist wanna be's to deal with that afternoon and I wasn't about to come back down there for anyone! So there!

I was to meet with a moving company at her house that afternoon for an estimate. *I sure was losing alot of work for her stuff* I thought to myself. I still couldn't believe that all this was happening. I was feeling pretty righteous and war-like because of the mornings 9/11 events when I got over there. I was making fun of the GTS in my mind. Comparing them to Osama bin Laden and his gang. Compared to *his* gang the GTS wasn't shit! *Why I could even blast them off the face of the planet and know one would even notice! Or maybe they would blast me off the planet and no one would notice that either!* I was thinking. I thought that alot during the next few days.

While I was waiting for the movers I was paid a short visit from the inbred hoodrat bitches. *What beautiful girls* I thought to myself as they chatted about how when the restraining order was up on Gabe, how he would be coming over to my house to claim what was his. How he was going to "busta cap" on me & stuff. How he was comin' to my "crib" with his "crew" to get his stupid dog that I didn't have. I knew I should have kept the damn dog so I could give it to him. If only he wouldn't have torn up the mystery puppy. I marveled at how stupid the gurlz were. Had they forgotten that I was a pistol packin' mama? Did I look like a push-over or some matronly fool that would take their shit? I'm not denying the fool thing, I am just saying.....

Anyway, I just tried to act disinterested in what they had to say since I couldn't think of a better response. They left when the movers showed up to do the estimate. Of course cell phones in hand, they stared out of the windows, wondering if Ray-Ray was really gone. Stupid bitches anyway. I agreed with the movers that Friday would be a good day to pack her things and put them in storage. I wished this situation would hurry and be over. Plus I wondered if moving day would be the day that the house would be shot up as predicted........ Shit. I still had to meet with the insurance lady on Thursday first for the break-in.

Our salon clients weren't happy that week. Hoochie was stuck in Boston because of Osama and his terrorist bullshit, and our new girl that I forgot to mention earlier was stuck in San Francisco. All of Tiny's clients were North Slope workers and were stuck on the North Slope.... As for me, I was gone so much due to local gangsters and my precious Ray-Ray's house, that I pissed off several clients who have never been back. I don't blame them of course, I only wish that they would have gone to the girls that were left at the salon. If they are reading this, maybe they will feel differently. Maybe not. I don't give a shit anyhoo!

Thursday came and I had to most definitely air the place out! Man what a stench! I didn't want the insurance lady to be overcome with asphyxiation from leftover cat box fumes. Big Daddy had dumped it when he came over to board the window but it still smelled! Hmmm.. Could have been the booby trap that smelled....... Anyway, the insurance lady came and went. After her visit I set about my next chore. Some house cleaning was in order.

As I stood there, I realized that I didn't really want to clean up all the crap there. I would have to hire a cleaning company! Man, what a mess! There was so much trash! And dirty dishes! Cat and dog food strewn everywhere! Pizza crust on the floor with dog shit! Gangsters certainly are messy people. I have to say though, most of the big mess came from the break-in frenzy. There was no excuse for the cat box and dog turds though. So I figured that I would just try to get most of the big throwaway stuff out of there for the dump. Which is how I became "friends" with the inbreds. One girls junk is another gurlz treasure! And what treasure Ray-Ray had! At least in the bathroom anyway!

There were gobs of hair products from Mercury and from bargain stores. There were imitation perfumes, dozens of bottles (empty and half full) of lotions, potions, assorted generic medications, moldy corroded styling tools, and cat litter!

Cat litter? *What was with that girl anyway?! Did she just let the cats shit wherever they pleased?* Towels covered the floor, soaking up a leak under the sink. *Turn off the water for the love of God!!!!*

Slaving in that disgusting bathroom, I had worked up a powerful thirst so I left to get a soda. Upon my return I discovered one of the gurlz sifting through the bathroom trash on the front porch that had become a treasure chest. She didn't waste much time. She actually was working up a sorting pile, dividing up the different types of beauty items. Just like a packrat! Hoodrats are packrats! Heh heh heh.. "Something interesting in there Greeny?" I asked as she jerked herself up from the mother lode. She grinned rather sheepishly at me and sauntered on down to me.

"I was jus' lookin' at whut you was throwin' out." she said in her best behavior voice. "You know whut? You n' me got off to the wrong start. Ahm' sorry fo that. You know? I was jus' thinkin' dat me an you could be frens'. You know? I was gonna axe you ifn' I could take some of dis' stuff, if you gonna throw it out." She smiled her most friendly smile. She looked like a clown in the freak show minus the makeup. Her green teeth were amazing as always. Then I figured that I would play her game. See what she had to say.

"I don't mind if you go through this stuff. You have already seen it. Just put back all the stuff you don't want. Ok?" I nodded the heads up nod at her and opened the door. She shuffled in after me. I watched her. Her eyes got big as she looked around the room.

"I got some baby stuff here I want. Is that ok?" she asked. "You know whut? I know who it was, broke into her house. Took the TV an some other stuff." She cracked a sideways glance at me. She was trying to get on my good side. I already knew who had broken in.....

"Yeah? Who? I think it was Gabe is what I think." I said. She was right into

I Just Wanted To Go Fishing !!!

following me everywhere. Almost like a little kid trying to be extra helpful.

"Yup. It was Gabe. Two other people. Vee too. She wanted her CD's. Dey threw a log through da window." It was funny the way she talked. It was regular English mixed with gangster talk and the more she said the more humorous and clown-like she seemed. She was trying so hard not to sound gangstery. If I answered her *gangstery* she would start off sounding gangstery. "Gabe? He's comin' to your house. He know where you live. He says you have a nice pad. He say he's comin fer Cobain. He might even rob you. I tole Ray dat he weren't no good. I use to date em. He say he's gonna shoot up yer house. Maybe even kill you. Soon as the restraining order you got is up, he's comin'. " She finished that last sentence looking quite please that she had divulged a secret to me, therefore gaining my trust.

"Yeah?" I said in my most gangstery accent I could imitate. "I have a message for you to give him. You tell him to C'MON MUTHAFUCKA! C'mon! He don't know my game! Tell him I gotta surprise wait'n for him with his name all over it in every window! Tell him if he come to my house, ah'll peel a cap on im' so big, it'll blow his fuckin' head clean off! Tell im' to C'MON with his bad self! I'm lookin' forward to it! I'm tired of him thinkin' he's all that. He ain't shit!" Greenie's eyes were huge. She was getting excited.

"Whachu got in da widow's?" she asked breathlessly. Her eyes were sparkling with delight. She didn't ask about the gun I would use to peel off a few caps with. She already knew that I had guns.

I ignored her and kept talking. "Yeah. You tell him I don't have his dog and if he comes to my house, I WILL kill him. I don't even care. He makes threats against me and mine? He doesn't know who he's fuckin' with. And if for some reason he makes it past me, Big Daddy will flay him alive Now I'm done talking about this to you. If you want some of this stuff, go ahead on it." Then her mother came over to visit and I cut that short saying that now Greenie wasn't bothering me, and that she had my permission to take whatever treasure her grubby little hands could find. What a repulsive family.

The insurance lady came and went. Her visit was uneventful. The movers came and went. Big Daddy came back from a successful hunting trip and took all Ray-Ray's trash to the dump. He's good like that. Then the cleaning lady came and went. No big shootout.

The pictures that Ray-Ray promised to send me finally came. What a good looking group of individuals. NOT!! Wow! The FBI was also waiting for the pictures. I had told them about them the day we were at her house. They were particularly interested in the group shot taken after the retaliation for the theft of Ray-Ray's dog. (The picture might have been taken after the crew jumped in a new member - I am not sure.) After making several copies for myself I turned them over to Officer Ryan on September 17. We talked about the restraining order. How it was only good for two more days. How I was scared that he would come to my house. How Greenie said that he would be coming over. That's all it ever was with me and Officer Ryan. Just talk. He was always trying to make me feel better. But the FBI had bigger fish to fry. Osama and friends. I hoped that if they ever found Osama, they would blow him off the face of the planet.

Chapter 9

Watchin' Our Backs

At the salon each day was the same. How my family was doing was the big question. How was Ray-Ray. How was Big Daddy? Are there really gangs in Anchorage? I didn't care if I ran reports, made coffee, cut hair or anything. I DIDN'T FREAKIN" CARE. I just wanted to take my kids and move my household, or go fishing and never come back!

And every day I explained to the clients who wanted to know, how it felt to wonder every day if the gangsters were watching you. I probably should have kept my mouth shut. I would have retained my clients..... But they asked so I told.....

Ever wonder what it feels like to speculate every day whether your kids are safe? I mean really safe. Not whether they were safely walking home from school as expected. You know, where being safe means staying out of the road, watching for cars. Or not jumping on trampolines without parental supervision. Or not climbing on the counter tops in search of a snack after school. All that stuff is basic behave-yourself-to-be-safe stuff.

My kids had to learn to watch for strange cars that might be full of teenagers parked in front of the house or maybe just driving by. They had to learn to look for perfectly folded blue head bands. All kids know to never talk to strangers. At least they are supposed to learn that at a young age. My kids weren't even allowed to talk to other kids their own age that they didn't know. You never know, they could be new GTS members. Did you know that the average shooter for a gang is twelve years old? I learned that.

Each day that I drove home from work, I always looked in my rearview expecting to see gangsters. Still do. Everyone was a suspect. Every car that turned the same direction *was* following me. I knew it. So I would make all sorts of detours to make sure that I wasn't. Then after I got home I would think about how stupid that was because the gang already knew where I lived anyway. Later I was told that they would drive by three times a week to check out my pad.... Gabe even went to my back yard to look for Cobain the pitbull. I knew this much to be true because he described my dog to me.

After each family outing, upon arriving home, I would sneak through the house. Listening for any strange sound. Watching the cats for nervous behavior. Looking for any items that may have been moved.

Big Daddy removed all his hunting rifles and put them at a friends house for safe keeping. It wouldn't be good to be shot with your own gun.

I knew Gabe would be coming to pay me a visit. I had messages from the gurlz didn't I? I was warned by the cops, both regular and FBI wasn't I? He knew where I lived. That was enough for me. I figured that maybe I should go hunting for him. Maybe capture him. Maybe lure him somewhere where he would attack me and then I could kill him. These were my murderous thoughts.

My middle daughter wrote an answer to the classroom assignment of what their scariest moment was. Her's was when she found out her sister was in a gang, and that she did drugs, and that the gang leader wanted to harm her family for retaliation. So how did that feel? Now that I know what I know about the GTS, I'm certain that coming over to busta cap on us would not be a problem

Meanwhile Ray-Ray got on with her life. She was safe. Although that was a good thing, I damned her every day. How could she place us in this position? What would happen? Maybe nothing. Hopefully nothing. Soon enough we would find out. The day was coming in a few days when the restraining order would be up. I would take off early for the occasion. Maybe set some booby traps. Yep, September 19 was coming up quick!

Chapter 10

Gangster Granny!

September 19, 2001 was a particularly boring day at the salon. The only real excitement we had was when we had to escort a psychotic hairstylist wanna-be outta there. (Psychotic Hairstylist Wana-be: A salon client who thinks he or she knows everything about hair, and wants to prove it by using the salons tools. Not good.) We had gotten rid of our token male stylist Mr. Schmoozie, and there were just four of us left to close up the beauty shop. Tiny had captured a "boy" for her amusement and was beautifying herself for the occasion, Lil' Dancer was teaching dance lessons, and Hoochie was off early to work at the House Of Ill Repute where she was a better waitress than a hairstylist. I too was intentionally planning on leaving early, for this was the day that Gabe would have access to my house without fear of going to jail. At least he would feel that way.

    I said my fare thee well's, and set off on foot for my parking spot. As usual I looked over to the transit center to admire the various characters that peddled drugs and whatnot there.

This day there were several skate boarders doing tricks, groups of young girls huddled together, the usual drunks, the long haired homeless guy that always juggled sticks (which was very cool by the way) and a couple of guys in blue headbands.

Blue headbands. Big deal. Hmmm. Wait! No one ever wears their colors downtown. Hmmm. I had better check this out! One of the guys walked with quite a swagger and it struck me that he looked like he would be friends with Gabe. Except that his hair was too long. But still. And how neatly his rag was folded! Pressed looking - starched even. I marveled that the other guy's was the same. They both turned to look at me wondering why I was looking at them. I just kept going and got in my car pondering the blue headbands.

As I started to pull out of the parking lot, I noticed a couple of other little bastards with the same style fold. They were obviously making a statement there for all the rest of the bus-stop folks. But what? I pulled out and drove over to the right lane. I saw even some more of them! There were packs of them everywhere! But the original two were staring at me and we all locked eyes. My stomach knotted up and I felt adrenaline as I stared them down.

There is a stop light a little ways down from there directly across from the salon. I knew it was coming so I tore my eyes from them and SLAM!! I had to hit the brakes! Quick! My friend Gabe barely missed getting run over by me! He was at my salon! I couldn't believe it. GABE! That bastard! We stared at each other and I rolled my window down as he backed away. "I wanna talk to you, you stupid fuckin' piece of white trash, mother fucker!" I yelled as loud as possible in my meanest voice. I wanted him to know that I meant business!

He tossed a few gang signs at me, which I threw back to him I noticed the sty on his eye was all healed up. He was still quite yellow and his stay in jail did nothing for his good looks. Poor guy needed some cosmetic surgery. Hands up high he yelled a quick "Fuck you bitch!", and took off running. The asshole was running away. Running away? Yep, that's what I said. Running away. Only his pants were so low that it was difficult which made him look comical! Some bad-ass, running away.

I dialed the salon and told Tiny to look out of the window. I asked her quickly if any of those yo-yo's were in the salon. She said no. Then I told her which one was my friend. She was rightly mortified. Gone were her plans of beautifying herself. Then I hung up on her.

I opened my door and started after him. The folks in the car behind me were honking at me to get the hell out of their way. Shit! Quickly I moved back into my seat and pulled over, yelling at him the whole time. He stopped once to shout and throw signs. No doubt the signs were telling me that I was dead meat or something. I told him that he was a cock sucking "P-word" with no balls and that he should come back. I was most definitely in a state of ass kickin' hysteria and was not my normal cautious self! Then two young girls started towards me with the obvious intention of shutting me up.

"C'MON! You stupid ugly bitches! C'mon! Tell that piece of white trash chickenshit that I'm gonna kill him!" I was hopping mad and feeling pretty righteous!

Then I thought of Officer Ryan. He said if anything *unusual*... Well this was unusual wouldn't you say? I dialed the number fast, still parked with Tiny watching in the window. It's a pager number so I was very pleased that he answered it so fast. "Officer Ryan! This is Mary O.! Gabe knows where I work! He is here right now and I'm gonna kill 'em! I'm tired of this shit!"

Investigator Ryan filled me in on how I should calm down, how I wasn't going to kill anyone, and then asked me where I was. I told him where I was, and that I most certainly *was* going to kill someone named Gabe, and that I would do it that night! He then told me to start driving to which I answered no I wouldn't, so he told me to drive again. And so I did. Slowly though I might add! Around the corner........

I told him that I was tired of not knowing where Gabe was, when he knew where I lived. I told him my new plan (crafted that very second) of how I would go make posters of the gangster photo. On the poster I would write in huge letters that I was watching him, and that I was waiting for him, and that if he wasn't too chicken shit to come see me, C'MON!, and then I would kill him. Yep! That sounded good. Real good. It didn't sound very good to Investigator Ryan though, and of course he said so. I argued the point for a second or so as I pulled over to the side of the street. I needed to park since after all, it can be dangerous to drive while talking on a cell phone. Plus I wanted to see if Gabe would come out from behind the building.

As I was getting ready for my next bit of arguing I spied a bit of blue coming towards me from the left. "Ho-ly shit! Here come some more of them! There's like six of them! What the fuck are all these guys doing here! Oh my God! Hey! Capone's with'em! What's he doing here? He told me he wasn't GTS!" (Remember? He was the cute Italian looking guy on the couch at Ray-Ray's house the day I was just supposed to be fishing.) Investigator Ryan asked me what they were doing, where they were going and I told him that they were coming towards me and that Capone liked me, and that he was smiling at me. I said that I was going to talk to him. He told me that would be fine and that he would like to listen and that he would send me some cops to watch over me. Cool! FBI snipers rock! Heh heh heh...

Capone walked up with two guys. "Yo! Waazzup Mary! How ya doin'?"

"Doin' good Capone." I said after the properly timed "yo's" and "wazzuup's"

I Just Wanted To Go Fishing !!!

were said. You see, when they say "yo", you say "yo" immediately after. The same with "waazzup" or "what up". "What's up with the blue headbands? What're ya doin' down here with Gabe? I thought you weren't bangin' with Gabe." I wanted to know the deal.

His huge black friend started over to the car. "Is dey' a problem ovah here? You got somethin' to say?" he asked. He was definitely not appreciative that I was asking questions. He came closer and I was getting a stomache ache - the kind where you might have to take a dump.

Capone put his hand up and stopped him. "Naw man. She's ma friend. You kin go. Yo Mary, where's ma hug?" He reached in and gave me a hug. I pretended to hang up my cell phone and put it on the dash.

You know what? I liked that kid. You'll remember that we bonded on the couch at Ray-Rays House O' Filth. He told me that Gabe was after me and that I should give him back his dumb dog. I told him the story about the dog and he said he was afraid for me and that I shouldn'a done that. He said that I shouldn't talk to Gabe and that if I did, there was no way that he could help me. I told him how I knew he would understand that the day I met him, and called the cops on him that I was just doing what any mom would do for family. That Gabe would *respect* that. Plus I was going to tell him about the dog. How I was going to tell him that I had no beef with him, but that if he came to my house I would kill him myself and be done with it. Better to do him before he did me!

Just then the black guy came back hollering that Capone had better get a move on. Gabe was pissed that he was talking to the bitch who was trippin' on him. I hollered then! You know I did! "You tell that piece of shit to stay there! You tell him that I wanna talk to him! You hold him there!" I gestured to Capone. He was all about No Way! So he shook his head, made the peace sign at me and hurried off. With his back to me I grabbed the phone and asked Investigator Ryan what to do. He said "Well go ahead and talk to him!" and I asked if I should call him back and he said he would like to listen, and I said that I would put him in my pocket. So with him in my pocket, and unseen FBI cops watching, off I went.

I fairly ran so he wouldn't get away. Once again I just knew FBI snipers were looking out for me. Whether there were any cops really looking out for me is anyone's guess. At any rate, I was fired up! Here he came, in all his gangster glory, all swaggering, and flinging his arms around like he does. "YO! GABE!" Said I.

"YO! Waazzuup?" Said he, to which I replied, "What izzz?" My stomach hurt so bad. I just knew that I would have an accident and embarrass myself just when I really needed to look extra tough. Plus my legs had sudden like, turned to rubber.

"I jus' want ma dog back. You got Cobain. I don't got-n-y beef wich-u. Sept fo' ma dog. Give'm back to me an' I got no problem wich-u. Aw-ite?" When he talks he dips his head to the side and down quite a bit although his eyes never waver. His hands are always moving. Not nervous hands. *Talking hands.*

"Yeah Gabe? That's not what I hear. I hear you're coming to my house to kill me and rob me. Here's the deal. I don't even know you. I don't have a problem with you except when you make threats against me and my family. You know? I don't have Cobain either. That damn dog killed the puppy of the bitch you were doing at Ray-Ray's house while she was working!" I said.

He says, "You know about that?" I say "Yeah, I know about alot of things".

He says, "Cobain killed that dog? You fo' real? You know, Cobain wuz a fightin' dog. I use ta fight 'im fo' money. He kicks ass! To the pound huh? Aww, tha's aw-rite. I don't have anyplace to keep 'im anyway. Why you call the po-leece on me? I didn't do nothin' to you. 'Cept call you names. Me an' Ray was fightin' the night before about me meetin' you. She say I can't meet you and I say why. She say she don' want you to know my game. Tha's why we was fightin. I wasn't beatin' her or nothin'. Is she still pregnant?"

WOW! He was talking to me! I couldn't believe it! This was very cool. I say, "I don't know shit about Ray-Ray! You know me and her. She told me that she lost the baby. Maybe she did. Maybe she didn't. I don't know. I don't know why she didn't want me to meet you either. She doesn't talk to me. All I know is that when she called me that day , I thought you were a weirdo who was beating her up and so I went over there to kick your ass! 'Cuz I'm her Mom you know, and I know you will respect that. You are better off without her. She doesn't appreciate nothin'!" That made him laugh out loud. A big laugh with his hand to his chest! My legs felt like rubber. I thought to myself how nerve wracking this was. It was hard not to crap on myself.

He says, "Yeah? She don't appreciate shit! You know her dog Doja? You still have Doja? Well, this dude took her dog cuz' she fucked up a deal (drug deal), so I take the crew over there and got him back. I beat the dude with his own gun! Took the drugs, the money, the gun, Doja, and went back to our house. She tol' me she didn't want the gun but the bitch was the firs' one under tha house to shoot it!"

"WHAT?!" I say. I didn't know about the clandestine target practice under the house. Shit! I remembered the cop in my pocket and tried to maneuver the pocket closer so he could hear Gabe confessing about the gun. "I know about the drugs. Whatever. Gun? What kind of gun? More than one gun? Why do you guys need guns?" I made sure to sound excited for the "gossip".

He filled me in on how she would target practice with a Tech 9, and a Deuce 5 under her house. How she set up a target and some suitcases to hide behind in case of a ricochet. He said she was a stupid bitch (no disrespect meant) for shooting under the house. Man! What would I hear next? I made a mental note to ask her about that. Then I asked if the guns were still there because I didn't want to "find" anything strange when the movers came, and that I wanted to make sure that he got everything that was his so that we didn't have a problem. He said no. Then he told me how he was only going to sleep with her when he first met her, and that he fell in love with her. He said all this rather sheepishly too I might add. YUK! He said that he was so glad to meet me and that he had no problem with me. We talked about how the white trash neighbors of hers were a pain in the ass. He said he wished he could have met me sooner and that he knew all along that we would get along and that we could have been fishing buddies.

He said, "I like you. I knew you was cool." I told him that I had to get home and make dinner.

He said he would see me around, that we were cool with each other, and that he had no beef with me, and if he heard if that triflin' Ray-Ray was pregnant, he would let me know. Holy BaJeeeezzzus! With that he gave me a huge gangsta hug, smiled a bright gangsta smile and started walking his gangsta walk. He turned around and threw peace and I love you signs at me and rounded the corner. (The love signs were interpreted for me by Ray-Ray)

Let me tell you! I couldn't get to my car fast enough. I wanted to run. I wanted to scream but knew I had to wait until I got into the car. I wondered aloud if my freakin' cell phone was still on. I unlocked the door and got in, closed the door. Whipped out the cell phone, and into it I yelled, "OH MY GOD! I GOT HUGGED BY A GANGSTER! DID YOU HEAR ALL THAT? AAAAAAH-HHH!!! I NEED TO TAKE A SHOWER! I'M SLIMY WITH GANGSTER SLIME! AAAAAHHHH! Ok. So did you hear all that? Did you hear about the guns? Are you still there? AAAAAAAAHHHHH!! Is this fucking phone on???"

Investigator Ryan did hear all that. In fact he recorded the whole thing. He said it was beautiful! He loved it. He was pleased to say that he thought I was safe for now. He was certain that I was in good with Gabe, which meant that I was good with everybody. Cool. He said to keep in touch, to call him if I heard anything from Gabe, made a few jokes about me being a secret informant, and then we hung up.

I went home and told my family the good news. I was in good with Gabe. In good with the GTS because I was in good with the leader. He (Gabe) actually told me later on that there were three black gangsters with him that day who wanted to "jack" me for trippin' on him. He said that no one touches his baby's Granma. They need to have respect.

A month went by and I hadn't seen Gabe downtown again. I wondered about him. I wondered if he looked at my house. I heard that he had driven by from Ray-Ray. She had been cooperating with Investigator Ryan and had been talking with Gabe. They made three way calls together and she had to confess to Gabe that she was still pregnant. That was the only way the handsome fellow would talk to her. If she wasn't pregnant then he had nuthin' to say to her. Investigator Ryan was hoping that she would be able to get more information from him

Speaking of that, did I mention that I wasn't supposed to tell Ray-Ray that he was FBI? Well, I wasn't supposed to so I didn't. He had her thinking that he was befriending her. She was eating out of his hands! Anything he wanted to know, she told. Which was good because she could have went to the Big House too. Which is what I thought should happen at the time, once I started finding out everything. Lucky for her that she cooperated! I told her if she didn't, she would be one of those jailbirds who have babies in prison and that I wasn't into raising a baby. Although I would have.

Anyway, like I said, I hadn't seen or heard from him which in a way was a good thing. But the bad thing was that Investigator Ryan was always telling me that it was going to take time. How much time is what I always wanted to know. I wanted this deal to hurry up and be over! For the love of God anyway! As usual

Mary Oyster

I was thinking these things as I started the drive home.

October here is Alaska is always cold and dark. The bright spot is Halloween which is one of my favorite holidays. I pondered on the drive home from the salon that first week of October, on how the next weekend our salon would have a haircutting class with a stylist from New York. She was alot of fun before and I was thinking about how we would all go haunted housing together. As I stopped at the first stoplight at "C" Street, I noticed a lone hunched up figure on the opposite side. He looked cold. Haa! 'Twas Gabe! *I believe I shall see waazzuup*, I thought to myself.

Pulling over to the side, window rolled down I yelled "YO! GABE!" and he strolled over to see who I was. He looked rather nervous. "Yo Mary. Waaazzzup!" said he.

"Get in. I wanna talk to you. What are you doing standing out here by yourself?" I figured he was waiting for a ride somewhere.

"Shiiit. I jus' got outta jail. Them foo's arrested me fo' a bad tail-light. My crew is s'posed ta come git me. You gotta cell phone I kin use?" said he.

"Yeah, you can use my phone." He made a quick call to cuss out whomever in the crew was supposed to meet him. Then he said, "Yeah, I been wantin' ta talk to you. You know Ray-Ray's pregnant? I wazn't sure you know. Do you know anythin' 'bout her talkin' to the cops? The fed's is after me. But dey don't have any ev'dence. They still be askin' me about some robbery an' shit."

I nodded my head and answered that I did know that she was pregnant. But that I also knew something that he didn't. You see, if you give him a tidbit of info, he will give back some. I was working him. "You are having a boy." That got him! Boy, did his eyes sparkle. Like a small child who got his first bike. Sparkly eyes on a thug. It was trippy because it was only for a second. A fleeting second I might add. "Hey, and what robbery? That Spenard Hotel one?" I added.

I Just Wanted To Go Fishing !!!

He ignored the robbery question. "A boy? Fo' real? Why hasn't she called me lately? How come she call you? You guys don't talk." That last sentence was spoken matter of factly.

I explained to him that she had been in the hospital with terrible appendicitis, had surgery and wasn't doing well. Most of that was true. Except that she was doing better and that the baby was A-ok. We drove around the block together. I should say, "rolled" around the block. While we were chatting with plenty of yo's being said, I asked him what the GTS crew was doing hanging out downtown all the time, and how I was tired of everyone staring at me with the Evil Eye while I walked to my car. He said they were down there letting everyone (other gang-bangers) know that they "owned" the downtown. He said that if he needed money, he would "tax" them for being there. He also said that he would let everyone know that they should show his baby's granma some respect or they could stay da fuck away from downtown! Now how do ya like that! Then he said that the feds had no proof that he robbed a motel. Just ouuta the blue, like that. So of course, we all know that he did do the robbery.

And with that, we could see the crew lounging about the entrance of the world famous Mercury Studio, and so he told me to honk, which I did. They all turned at once to see who had the balls to honk at them and that is when he gave me my second gangster hug. It wasn't as slimy as the first one. Then he said, "Peace", and walked away. All the gangsters were staring and he turned, made peace signs, and some other signs, and then they all hugged him, and off they went. *Better call Officer Ryan. This was unusual right?! Right?*

I like visiting with Officer Ryan. He's rather funny. He said that he was the one that arrested Gabe, and that he was so pleased that we seemed to have "bonded" so well. "Well Mary, sounds like you are an Honorary Member of the GTS! Wow! He could have been your son-in-law!" he joked. Too funny, that guy. Son-in-law... Grim.

That week I started to get asthma again. It never fails. GTS, Ray-Ray, and asthma go hand in hand. Back on the steroids, gettin' chubby again. Shit. I couldn't really afford to get Steroid Induced Flab since it might be necessary to bust out with my wrestling moves! Don't laugh, you never know when a Stone Cold Stunner might come in handy. I saw GTS members every day at the transit center. They usually came around 4:00pm. I think that is a normal time for pretty much all gangsters. Sort of a morning time seeing as how they all work nights. Heh heh heh heh.... Anyway, extreme stress gives me the Terrible Asthma (different from Regular Asthma), and the gangster presence in the close vicinity of the salon was definitely stressful. Blue headbands everywhere. Jeez! So off to the hospital I went again for treatments and steroids. Packin' on the pounds after that, I was! I was off work for two weeks that time. Quite the drag really. Then the Jailbird Phone-calls started.

You know how everyone who wants to call you seems to know what time you sit down to dinner? Or just walk in the door? Or get ready to play a board game with your children? Or knows that you have call waiting so they keep calling? Well, that particular month (October-November) telemarketers for charity, Ray-Ray and Gang Leader Gabe all vied for the phone time. Not a day went by when two of three of them would call two or three times per night. "Wait! Don't answer the phone!" I would gasp in between nebulizer treatments. "Check Caller ID!" I hang up on all telemarketers. Maybe not answer Ray-Ray's calls for fear of being stuck listening to her tales of woe. Maybe answer the Jailbird Call if I was in a charitable mood, or depending on how much medication I had to take. The phone calls came when he was in jail, which is how I would know if he was out or not.

Anyway, my Gangster Friend was in and out of jail several times. Put in by you know who, Officer Ryan. He just kept picking away at Gabe and his friends.

Waiting for him to confess? I don't know since that is privileged FBI info. (I would sure dig a ride at night with the cops arresting gangsters. I was going to be a cop once, back in 1984 you know. Even took the written test, but chickened out on the rest of the tests because everyone I knew told me that if I became a cop, I would be a bad mother to Ray-Ray. Hmm... Maybe I shouldn't have listened to them.) Yo!

One phone call was in December. Back in jail again! He was distraught that he didn't know I had been in the hospital again while he was out of jail. That, and he was wondering if I would be his third party custodian. As if! He said, "Yo, I didn' know dat shit. You was in da hospiddle? If I woulda known, I would'a came ta visit. Bring you some flowers an' shit. I would take care of you cuz' you my baby's Granma! Me'n ma gurl woulda came ta see ya. You ma fren' an' shit!" Now that would have been something! Can you imagine? Gangsters in the pulmonary ward. Good God! That would have been a little much, and the next day when I told the story to my fabulous client Shelly, she agreed. Then she promptly named me Gangster Granny, which is how I got my name.

Gangster Granny. Hmmm. has a nice ring don't you think? NOT! *Gangster freakin' Granny*! I had all sorts of imaginings of when I would finally meet my grandbaby (who still wasn't born at the time). *Come to Gangster Granny, my little Gangster Baby, kiss kiss, smoochy smoochy!* Gaaawwd! Shelly even calls to make hair appointments asking for Gangster Granny. It stuck! I just want to be The King again! Maybe even The Bumble Master! But no! I have become Gangster Granny, Honorary Member of the GTS. Officer Ryan loves it. Thinks it funny. Is happy that we have "bonded" so well.

Gabe and I bonded so well that I can walk into the crowd of gangsters and wanna-be's, knowing that no one can bug me. One night after work, I had a couple of wanna-be gurlz body slam me in the elevator, so I slammed them right back!

This was after they shoved a lady who wasn't overly assertive and quite frumpy into the wall. One quite unattractive gal with her headband tied in a disrespectful mess (by GTS standards anyway), asked me what my problem was. So I say "Yo bitch! Did your mama teach you to disrespect your elders? Apologize to this lady!" She said a loud disrespectful remark such as fuck you or something, and pushed me again, so I shoved into her hard enough to turn her around. Then I told her that if she chose to become violent with me, that she was choosing to fuck herself severely. With that she glared and stomped off. She'll think twice about doing that again! Yeah right. Next time she'll probably pull a knife and stab me with it. Hmmm. I really should leave well enough alone. I was after all getting ready to turn forty. Forty? For the love of God! Forty, a grandmother, and gangsters. What next? I need to remember sometimes that my personal bad-ass days are most definitely over!

Anyhow, one day after parking my car in the treacherous parking garage (which be the way, is jinxed and has had it's share of violent crimes committed in it, including murder), I arrived behind the transit center on foot, like every other day. Who did I see? Gabe! All cuddled up to his new girlfriend. Yuk.. What a prize! She had some serious ghetto blonde hair, seriously painted eyebrows, sorta like a drag queen on crack! Looking around I could see that she and Gabe were obviously the royalty of the bus stop! Since he didn't see me I thought I would mess with him and interrupt his little love fest. You know, crash the party. There were all sorts of gangstery characters in there including the two girls from the elevator. Hmmm.. This could be rather amusing.

Bang! Bang! Bang! I knocked on the window. First he reared back with a look of fury but quickly changed his tune when he saw my friendly face! His gurl didn't look very appreciative of me though, and neither did the rest of the bunch. She was loudly inquiring who that stupid bitch was, and he loudly yelled to all that

I Just Wanted To Go Fishing !!!

I was His Baby's Granma, and to show some respect! That did it. Everyone was quiet as I walked in the door and over to him. The elevator girls however stood up and tried to make a big show of keeping me from him. I said "Excuse me!" and they moved and followed. I walked over to him and he said "Yo! Wazzzuup Mary!" And I said "Yo Gabe! What izzz?" And then I looked at his New Gurl and told her that I was going to borrow "her man" for a minute if she didn't mind. She said that she didn't mind which was bullshit because she said it with slanted eyes and her nose was flared, painted eyebrows raised. Hmmmph!, I thought to myself as I extended my arm for him to properly escort me outta there. Too funny! He linked his arm with mine and sheepishly walked me out. Ha! That'll show them. Right? Yep. Tha's right.

We had a nice little chat about how things were going well for him. How Ray-Ray was getting big. Whether or not he would be allowed to be a part of the baby's life. That sort of thing. Then I asked him about the elevator girls being so disrespectful and he said he would take care of it because nobody disrespects his baby's Granma. Then he gave me my third gangster hug and off he went back inside. Those girls never bothered me again, and everyone in the bus stop all said waazzuup! to me whenever we ran into each other. Which was pretty much every day for a couple of months.

Gangster Granny. What a name! Better than being Dead Meat. But still, when the heck was Officer Ryan going to be done investigating? Jeeez. I was tired of playing the game. Tired of my clients all seeing the blue headbands. Just tired. Tired of everyone telling me that I should quit talking to Gabe. What? Are you crazy?, I would say or think. There was no way that I was going to piss him off. Him or his beautious girlfriend.

The rest of December and January for Gangster Granny were fairly quiet. I just didn't answer the calls. The Terrible Asthma only visited me once at Christmas. And then I knew that my friend was not in jail because the phone calls stopped. I knew that he was layin' low. Stayin' out of trouble. At least with the law. He was actually quite busy robbing prostitutes of their drugs, playing bingo, smoking crack and taking crystal meth with his girlfriend. Mmmmm mmm, what a fine individual! Could have been my son-in-law..........

Officer Ryan assured me that he was trying his hardest. He had to get hard evidence. I was losing faith.

Chapter 11

Da Phone Iz Ringin'!

These are the scribbled notes of phone conversations with Gabe. Some of the sentences will seem really garbled, but that is how he talks when he is excited. I have left them the way he says them so you can see how sometimes it is hard to decipher what he says. I mentioned to him that I was writing a book. Officer Ryan arrested him sometime in January, and thwarted a future robbery. So the phone calls really started coming. They were always fifteen minute conversations because that is all the time allowed for him to talk per call. The funny thing was, he seemed to have unlimited calls and would call two or three times in a night to finish a story.

When the phone would ring (at the time), and I could see on caller ID that it was Evercom Systems, I would get all nervous and sometimes have asthma. Should I pick it up and press zero to take the call? Should I not answer it? If I pressed zero, where would I go to talk to him? The answer to that would be in the bedroom so nobody (Big Daddy and kids) could hear me. So they wouldn't see me nervous and scared that I would say the wrong thing. And so that they couldn't hear me play the word games with him as I tried to learn and understand what he was talking about. And most of all, so they couldn't hear me laugh at some of the stuff he talked about. Sometimes when he talks it is super funny, and I don't know why.

Plus it was also nerve wracking that I felt that I was being sucked in to Gangsterville in a weird way. If I was rude and hung up on him, then I would piss him off and he could send over a crew member. I was terrified of that. At the same time, I found him fascinating. Anyway, here are the scribbles.

2/6/02 Talked to Gabe. He told me about being 5 years old and changing his baby sister's diapers. That his mom went to prison when he was 6. Joined a gang at 8. Was given his 1st gun at 13 by the leader of his gang (main homey) At 13 1/2 he was in a park & a carload of rival gangsters drove up and pulled a gun & Gabe pulled his gun out and started shooting, and he ran while he was shooting. He ended up shooting some kid who lived. He served 5 years at McLaughlin for that. During that time he got his high school diploma, and I imagine he got meaner & meaner. He told me about retaliation for Ray-Ray where he beat up the guy that took her dog. He told me about meeting her. He met her sometime in early spring or late winter. Partied with her. He finally tells her in June sometime that he should be her man so they "do their thing", and he moved in 2 days later. He becomes disenchanted with her because she becomes bossy and the rest of the gang thinks she is stuck up. Only now she is pregnant. He says he should have listened to her more because maybe he wouldn't be in jail. He said she was too self righteous and that is why he got tired of her. She was always telling him to be a man. (To him being a man meant taking care of business.) To her being a man meant kissing her ass.

It is good to have a woman to put money on the books - Gabe

2/7/02 Tonight talked to Gabe. He told me his philosophy on raising pitbulls. That was started because he says he wanted his dog Cobaine back. You have to be mean with pits to teach them respect and them after beating the shit outta them, pet them. Sometimes you have to punch them in the face to make them listen. How he loved Cobain and that he wouldn't listen to Ray-Ray but that he would protect her. How he would drink coffee and smoke cigarettes in the morning on the porch, and watch Cobain play. Told me he drove by our house at least 3 times a week and said that I had a big ugly dog (bullmastiff) but that she & Cobain would have bmade cool puppies. Told me that the day I confronted him on threatening me, the black guy that asked if I had a problem, he told Gabe I was some lady " be trippin' on Gabe" and the black guy had 2 other friends and at one time they all had "beef" wid each otha, and den all was cool and that they wanted to back him up and 'jack" me and he tole em to not touch me cuz tha's mah baby's granma. So he wouldn't let anyone touch me and all were to have respect for me. Heh heh heh He wants me to third party him. Third party? Yeah right.

03/01/02 He is pissed off at the feds. The mu-fuckers tryin' to get him to rat on his brother and fren's. Was offered 35 years to talk. Says I shouldn't have listened to the cops - that he would have never harmed me or Ray Ray - never harm a woman except that awhile back he broke his girlfriends jaw 'cuz she wuz pregnant and she lost the baby cuz she wuz smokin' crack and was triflin' with him.. He was comin' off his own drugs so he lost his mind and cracked her in the jaw. (he felt it was righteous anyway since she was smoking crack while pregnant with his baby) (Never harm a woman???) Have I thought about third partying him?

03/02/02 Gabe is "jus' gonna enjoy the kickback time in da pretrial phase. Da feds is tryn' ta fuck up da freedom. He will tell me everything & give me the discovery papers if I go to see him. He still wants me to third party him. (Which I never did.) Check dis out! *He always starts sentences with that. Yo!*

03/05/02 Feds think they pretty slick. *He can't tell me everything. He will tell me when I come to visit.* Everyone in his family is in trouble. I told him that he would become someone's "special friend" in prison and he said that - if dey wanna pump him, dey havta beat his ass first. He will be a loner for his time. Stay away from everyone. He will be like "Menace 2 Society" for his time regarding his girlfriend (*whatever that means-guess I should watch the movie or listen to the CD whichever it is*). His whole adult family has done federal time. He says his sister Jenny was wearing a wire the whole time Ray knew her (I found out later that he was exaggerating a bit). It was her boyfriend Crim Alexie that was shot during the last robbery. She thinks that Gabe & Ian set that up cuz they didn't like him - he was a punk. Gabe says Crim has a mind of a 10 year old. He is looking at 57 years. *He has a good point as far as this one- child molesters, rapists and murderers don't get as much time as he is looking at. What's up with that?* He says that all he has on his "juvy" record is runnin' from the po-leece. He hopes that the baby has "our eyes" (meaning his & mine which are blue) He definitely thinks that I am his friend. In some twisted way I almost feel sorry for him. What a stupid fuck! He wanted to know what sort of guy her new boyfriend was. Was he handsome etc.. I told him that he was a bit dorky, and he said she went from a preppy buff dude, to wannabe thug, to dork. He wanted to name the baby Manual for a boy or Alena for a girl. He wants me to third party him. He wants to know if I see any of his crew on the streets.

03/06/02 Gabe called with "good" news. He was very excited (tickled almost) to tell me that his lawyer delivered to him "Motions" 1. to suppress Gabe's statements of 1/03/02 because of no Miranda Rights at first. 2. Motion to dismiss - illegal evidence 3. Separate trial for each robbery. He talked so fast that I couldn't begin to decipher what all he said. For as dumb as he sounds, he sure can read fast. Truly amazing. When he gets out he would like to go fishing with me. Shiiit!!!

Wants to know if he will be a part of the baby's life.

Officer Ryan is all over this! I talked to him tonight and told him what Gabe had to say & he said that an all cases pretty much that there will be motions. I asked him about the Beckett (Gabes brother Ian) thing in the paper about the poor Native lady that was raped & murdered. He tried to explain why the state can't give immunity unless the feds drop the case against him but I didn't understand. Officer Ryan thinks it's funny that I am Gangster Granny & is glad that Gabe & I have "bonded" so well. I also thanked him for keeping Rochelle (Gabe's girlfriend) away from me. He says that Jessica (Gabes sister) is in jail & that Rochelle is not staying with her as Gabe told me. Anyway he told me that Gabe was for sure going to federal prison & I need not worry. Yeah, we shall see.....

Got a letter to Ray-Ray from Gabe. He told me I could read it (like I hadn't already) He said he is sorry for messing up her life. Hmmm.. He said that he wanted to be a part of the baby's life because he knows what it is like to grow up without a father. (I need to check myself. I am starting to feel sorry for him. I too know what it is like to grow up without a father. Except that my father abandoned me when I was eighteen, not as a small child like Gabe's father.)

03/09/02 Gabe says he goes to court in May. Doesn't want to rat out his brother. Is holding out for a better deal. (I encouraged him to take the plea bargain. That way all the gangsters would be in jail I figured) Wants me to third party him. He tells me about when he got beat up real bad by six inmates who were retaliating on him because his brother wore a wire in a murder case. Hmmm... Wants me to come visit him.

03/10/02 - 03/31/02 Almost daily calls. Maybe I take them & maybe I don't. Wants to know if his girlfriend is bothering me. (she was) Wants to know if Ray Ray is here. Says he watches Judge Judy everyday. He says that if he can get out he will go to fight for his country - even get cloned for the feds to use as soldiers.

He will never drink or do drugs again. His eyes are wide open now. He regrets everything. *I bet he does!* Wants to know when the baby is coming. Wants me to come visit him.

04//02 No phone calls for a week. Then they started coming daily again. He is panicking about court. Asks if I see Capone or anyone else on the street. I tell him the baby was born and that he is healthy. Gabe is thrilled. He asks if his girlfriend is bothering me. Says not to tell her about the baby. Asks me to come see him. I tell him that his girlfriend threatened me and that I called the cops. *I didn't go visit him. I secretly wanted to but I was too scared. Plus I didn't want to see the fear in his eyes because he would become to human for my liking. A human being that although is violent, has emotion and feeling. I did not want that.....*

Chapter 12

Court Full Of Gangsters!!

Memorial day 2002 was on it's way! The only problem with this Memorial Day was that I would also be turning 40. Forty freakin' years old! How traumatizing! I would be a forty year old grandmother, and that did not sit well with me. Plus my Fishing Partner was calling me King Grandmother in his Southern accent and it was starting to get to me. He would even call the salon and ask for Granny Oyster! BAD! BAD! BAD! So since he felt sorry for me, Big Daddy purchased me a beautiful 1973, 22 foot Terry Trailer Camping House (the Fish Mobile was dead). He was feeling so bad for me about being stared at by gangsters, and asthma, and being a forty year old grandmother and all, that he just felt inclined to make me very happy. But before fishing, we must go to court! This was promising to be a fine summer! But first court

May 6, 2002 was the start of the trial of the GTS. I was totally going to that don't ya know! Finally, after all the waiting, all the phone conversations with Gabe and other gangsters, it would finally be over. I had found out about court the Saturday before after talking with Officer Ryan. I had called him to tell him that Gabe's effervescent "fiancee" had called me to inform me that I had better stay away from her man. She thought I had gone to visit him with Ray-Ray. I wondered when the dumb bitch would quit asking me if she had moved back. I told her she was a stupid bitch and told her not to call me again. If she does, officer Ryan will haul her in for harassing a federal witness. I liked that. Federal witness.

Anyway, Gabe had made a plea bargain with the feds. It was something like if he testified against his brother Timothy Ian Becket (street name Romeo), he would receive a reduced sentence from 65+ years to only twenty-five or thirty-five. I am not sure which. I only know that I had encouraged him to do that during one of our conversations. (That way I figured all the gangsters would be in jail & I would be dead & gone when they all got out!) He was also to testify against two gang members named Raymond Theile and Daniel Troxel. I wondered if these guys were as unattractive as the other members of the crew I had seen. And wouldn't you know, they were way worse! Made Gabe look like Mel Freakin' Gibson! Not only were they hideous goons, but the family members that I sat amongst were even scarier! I was surrounded by inbreds! Gawd! I couldn't wait to tell the salon about this!

So the first day I went into the courthouse. It was a little nerve wracking looking at the guys in suits with earphones and guns. I couldn't imagine any bad guys getting past these guys that was for sure! They were standing there all stiff and unsmiling, and they all needed haircuts too I might add. After passing through the metal detector I went upstairs and waited in the lobby area for the doors to open. I was nervous and excited. I was going to hear Gabe confess and rat out his brother! Whooey!

In the courtroom, the audience was all dressed in their White Trash Finery that first day. You should have seen them! There were four young girls all with babies.

I Just Wanted To Go Fishing !!!

Gangster babies. GTS babies. I couldn't help thinking that this is where it all must start. If you are born into a gang, how do you know anything else? I was thankful that my grandchild was not there. I just knew that these moms would be loving to the babies, and later probably beat them or call them horrible names. Ray-Ray had told me how one of the girls (Gabes sister) treated her kids, and it wasn't good. She would call her baby girl such names as fuckin' bitch. Now why Ray-Ray allowed that in her presence I will never know. DFYS was on her ass all the time.

The grandmas and other relatives of these babies and gangsters were no better. There was one guy who was way scary to look at! I would never want to meet him in broad daylight much less in the backwoods where he was surely from. He had greasy long hair, beady eyes lined with sunken wrinkles caused from years of smoking probably, and he was wearing a filthy jacket. Ray-Ray probably would have said that he was "nice". She said that about all white trash individuals. His wife (I think) was dressed that first day in an old dress and had lanky, fine hair. You could tell she had a real hard life. Both of them reeked of cigarette smoke as did the rest of the audience.

I noticed right away that Officer Ryan needed a neck trim! Of all the things to notice. I was sure that his stylist wouldn't be happy with him for appearing in court with a fuzzy neck. He was probably too busy busting gangsters to worry about his hair judging from the size of the files!

Finally, the gangsters were all led out. They were all dressed nice - probably with clothing paid for by the taxpayers. Ian (Gabes brother) had on a turtle neck sweater to cover up his GTS tatoo on his neck. One by one, the girls would hold up their babies for the fathers (robbers, drug dealers, thugs...) to look at. I was in the twilite zone once again! How in the hell did Ray-Ray become involved with these disgusting humans? How disgusting does that make her? How sad. How much of this could be my fault? Now that I look back on her high school years, she always did hang out with white trash. I just thought she hung out with "alternative" kids. What a dumbass I am! What a bad mother I must have been! Who knows?

There was a girl with long red hair that I originally mistook for one of Gabe's sisters. She and Ian kept nodding at each other and at the other two guys. She had a daughter of about two years old. Gabe later said she was the girlfriend of one of the others. She gave me many Evil Eyes that week. All the girls did. (turns out that some of them thought I was a reporter) Only one girl was missing. Gabe's beautiful "fiancee". I was certain that she would be there the day he testified.

The jury selection took up the first day. They were mostly a bunch of puckered up conservative folks who held very conservative jobs. Imagine their shock at the gangsters! In Anchorage, Alaska? Gangs? They were scared just looking at them all. I couldn't wait for them to get a look at Gabe. When he looks mean, he looks mean! Anyway, they were all read the charges. Among the charges (not in order) were:

1. Interfering with international commerce by robbery.

2. Transferring a firearm in order to commit violence.

3. Conspiracy to commit armed robbery.

4. Brandishing a firearm.

5. Other stuff.

As the charges were read the gangsters would all wipe foreheads, cover mouths, write notes. Stuff that nervous people do. The jurists were all looking studious and hopeful that this wouldn't be a long trial. They all had other things to do. Jobs to go to, possibly fishing to do..... But no, they were all there to hear the wonders of the Anchorage Chapter Of The GTS.

I am pretty sure everyone in the courtroom was secretly fascinated with the inner workings of a gang. You could see it in their eyes as the information came. The disbelief that there was any truth in the story of a "gang" in Alaska. I think that the jury was thinking that "gang" was an exaggerated word used to make the case more sensational.. That was, until they heard all the testimony. After which I am sure that they all got in their little cars, back to jobs, back to their homes where they keep stories of badness from their children.

The jury was told how if a person wanted to join the *Good Boys Trece Serenos* (GTS) headed up by Gabriel Clark-Aigner (Casper) and Timothy Ian Becket (Romeo), then they would have to get "jumped in" first. Getting jumped in meant that the hopeful gangster wannabe would have to withstand a severe beating by members to show they "had heart". Their motto was that *"You're on your back now, but you'll never be again"*. Then after the beating, while still in pain with cracked ribs and such, the hopeful member had to do some "dirt". The dirt for some of the boys being the Spenard Motel robberies committed in January 2001.

The jury was told that the GTS got together on January 1st 2001 at a trailer to conspire with everyone to rob the hotel. The robbers would have use of two automatic handguns - one of which Ian owned. Gabe would be the backup guy and Ian would drive the getaway car. Crim Alexie wanted to be a GTS member, so he would be the robber after he got the shit kicked out of him. After the robberies the money would be split with the gang members who were at the trailer, after Gabe and Ian's cut of the spoils. Much partying would be done to celebrate the new member. We all got to watch a video of the robbery.

Two guns were used for the robberies. One was a 357 revolver and the other one was a 40 caliber semi-auto. I wasn't paying close enough attention in court (because I suck) to tell which gun was carried by which robber, I just know that the robber on the videos was holding a big black gun to the manager's head.

January 4, 2001 was the first big night. At first the dumbasses were going to rob the Millenium Hotel, but since there was a cop car parked outside they decided to go to a smaller location with more back roads for escape routes. At 3:14 am,

Gabe and Ian gave Crim the gun and commenced the first robbery. The video was extra grim for me, since I knew the robber in the back was my "son-in-law". (Some people still find it amusing to tease me about my "son-in-law even if he isn't really one) The manager of the hotel was an old man who kept his cool during the robbery even though he had a gun to his head, and had to listen to alot of severe cussing. He gave them all the money, and they left.

My own daughter slept with a violent, gun toting robber! And made friends with the rest of the gang!!! What the fuck!

The next two robberies were pretty much the same except that during the third, on January 30, 2001, the hotel owner had had enough, and happened to have a concealed weapon permit. So he shot the robber (Crim Alexie who was also in the first robbery) multiple times and then called 911. The 911 tape was played for the jury and it was more hideous than the videos because the owner was hysterical and didn't know if he had killed him. Plus, he was Asian and so talked really fast and sounded all the more hysterical. Meanwhile Gabe and Ian and whoever else escaped while their friend lay possibly dead or dying on the hotel floor. There was blood everywhere. I felt so sorry for that man for having to shoot someone. I would have done the same if I found the balls to do it. The gangsters all went back to the trailer and changed clothes, and then they all went back to the hotel, parked across the street and strained their eyes to see if Crim was dead. He lived, and isn't right in the mind according to Gabe.

(Why do you suppose Crim had to do the third robbery when he was already jumped in previously? I'll tell ya that later when the time comes. Just for a tidbit of insight into Gabe's justifications on things.)

When the 911 tape was played over and over again, all the gangsters and family members would cry. I mean *real* crying. Who would think that people who didn't care if the person being robbed was in fear of his life, (therefore showing total disregard for human life) could actually have *human* emotions and feelings? What a trip.

Well, let me tell you that by the time it was Gabe's turn to testify, whew! The jury was into it! They would all gasp and fidget. This shit was in everyone's backyard! After all, Anchorage is a small town!! Everyone was anticipating the entrance of Gabe. The leader of the GTS. From the looks on their faces, they were expecting a giant, hideous ogre. Probably covered with scars and stuff. They weren't expecting a person of medium build and height, hanging his head so low you could see the back of his neck. He had freshly shaved his head like he always does before going in front of a judge, because he thinks it makes him look more respectable. He doesn't realize that it makes him look more frightening to regular folks.

Gabe took the stand and couldn't speak. Couldn't look up. testifying against his brother and fellow gang members was more than he could bear. It was against everything in his entire being. Against all gang family rules and beliefs. He had no choice though. Either face over 60 years in prison, or plea bargain and get way reduced time. Ian glared at him the whole time and made a motion of cutting his throat while Gabe choked on his own sobbing words just to tell the court his name. I found myself pitying him. I thought that if someone in the audience tried to hurt him, I would help him. Wow! What a bond! Scary huh... There was so much hatred in the courtroom that day. I knew that if he escaped he would be beaten and killed.

The defense lawyers were trying to pick him apart. Trying to invalidate his testimony. He had first made a confession tape when he was first arrested claiming all blame to protect everyone, like a good gang leader would. I found myself silently rooting for him. Wishing that he wouldn't let them rattle him. I felt sorry for him. He was trying to sound so articulate, not like a gangster. The defense kept accusing him of lying. Finally he exploded! "Look foo'! You want me to tell the troof? If you want, I kin lie to you, tell you what you wanna hear." He looked like Eminem up there! Except mean and nasty! All gesturing and stuff!

The jury members all jumped back in their seats. Aghast! Scared! They thought he was going to jump out of his box, grab a gun, and start beating someone with it. The defense attorney broke out into a sweat and Officer Ryan looked as if he was covering a chuckle while wiping his forehead. It was beautiful! Gabe in all his gangsta glory told his version of the story which I believe was the truth. The jury thought so too.

May 13, 2001 the jury came back with a verdict for Timothy Ian Becket of guilty on all counts! Guilty! Guilty!

Guilty! He is getting like 57 years in federal prison. Yeah baby. Theile was guilty on 3 or 4 counts & Troxel walked. They still have state charges against them and Ian & Troxel are witnesses for the prosecution in the Joshua Wade murder trial. Of course Gabe and several of his friends are going away as well.

Officer Ryan and his friends all worked so hard for this day. I remember thinking that it would never come. Going to the salon every day, seeing the GTS outside the windows, walking through some of them to get to my car was over. Yay! Now I could go run the salon in peace and plan my upcoming Memorial Day fishing trip! Tiny, Lil Dancer and Hoochie would be so pleased to have a non stressed co-worker back. I was a bit of a lunatic during that time!

August 7, 2001 Gabe was sentenced to 25 years in a federal prison. Once again he had freshly shaved his head except for the tail that I don't think he will ever part with. I have told him several times that the tail would be used in prison by bigger, meaner prisoners as sort of a handle.

I Just Wanted To Go Fishing !!!

ANCHORAGE 8/8/02
Man who robbed Spenard Motel is sentenced to 25 years

A local man was sentenced Wednesday in U.S. District Court to 25 years in federal prison for his role in at least two robberies last year at the Spenard Motel.

Gabriel Clark-Aigner, 20, described as a member of a gang called Good Boys Trece Sorenos, pleaded guilty to two counts of robbery and two counts of using a gun in connection with a crime.

He faced nearly 40 years in prison, but Judge John W. Sedwick reduced the sentence by almost 15 years because Clark-Aigner cooperated with prosecutors.

He testified against fellow gang members during the May trial of Timothy E. Beckett, Raymond Thiele and Daniel Troxel. Beckett and Thiele were convicted by a federal jury on multiple robbery and gun counts. They are set to be sentenced later this month. Troxel was acquitted of the three charges against him.

Clark-Aigner also was ordered to pay restitution of more than $2,600 to the Spenard Motel.

During the sentencing hearing, Clark-Aigner wiped at his eyes and apologized.

"I still have a chance for a life," he said. "I'm gonna make the best out of it, change my life, you know."

— *Anchorage Daily News*

ANCHORAGE 8-30-02
Man convicted in Spenard Motel robbery sentenced to nine years

A U.S. District Court judge sentenced Raymond Thiele to more than nine years in prison for his role in robbing the Spenard Motel in January 2001, prosecutors said.

Thiele, 22, was convicted by a federal jury in May on one count of conspiring to commit robbery, one count of robbery and one count of brandishing a handgun. He was acquitted of two other charges.

Thiele was ordered to serve 111 months in prison and to pay restitution of $1,900 to the motel, said assistant U.S. attorney Dan Cooper.

A co-conspirator, Timothy E. Beckett, was convicted of 10 charges. He has not been sentenced yet. A third co-conspirator was acquitted of the three charges against him.

Prosecutors said the three were members of a local gang, Good Boys Trece Sorenos, that robbed the Spenard Motel.

— *Anchorage Daily News*

ANCHORAGE
Robber agrees to become a witness for prosecution in murder trial

An armed robber who had refused to testify in the Joshua Wade murder trial agreed Wednesday to become a prosecution witness in return for being allowed to serve two prison terms at the same time.

Timothy Beckett, 22, pleaded no contest in state court Wednesday to one count of first-degree robbery for his role in a January 2001 home invasion and assault at a Midtown trailer court. In return for his cooperation in several cases, including his testimony in the Wade trial, the state agreed Beckett's sentence in this crime can be served at the same time as a federal sentence for an unrelated hotel robbery.

The prosecution wants Beckett to tell a jury that Wade took him to see the body of Della Brown at a Spenard shack where her remains were eventually found by police. Wade is charged with raping and murdering Brown in early September 2000. His trial is set for November.

In addition, Beckett wore a police wire and engaged Wade in a conversation in which Wade seems to admit having killed Brown.

The prosecution's relationship with Beckett as a witness against Wade ran into trouble when he and a gaggle of other junior gangsters were arrested and charged with multiple counts of armed robbery by both state and federal prosecutors.

Because Wade's attorney would have been able to force incriminating admissions from Beckett about the robberies, Beckett exercised his Fifth Amendment right and refused to take the stand against Wade, forcing delay of the trial. Beckett gave up that right in the deal signed Wednesday and agreed to testify.

Assistant District Attorney John Novak asked that sentencing in both the federal and state robbery cases be set after the Wade trial to make sure Beckett holds up his end of the bargain.

— *Anchorage Daily News*

Mary Oyster

ANCHORAGE
Man sentenced to 10 years for role in two armed robberies

Gabriel Clark-Aigner was sentenced Friday to 10 years in prison for his role in two 2001 armed robberies. Clark-Aigner, 20, was part of a gang that committed several violent robberies in Anchorage, including a home invasion and assault at a Midtown trailer park in January 2001.

The 10-year sentence, handed down Friday in state court, will be served concurrently with a 25-year sentence imposed last month in federal court in a third case.

— *Anchorage Daily News*

Wired informant testifies at Joshua Wade murder trial

■ **BECKETT:** Defense takes on prosecution witness today.

By SHEILA TOOMEY
Anchorage Daily News

Jurors in the Joshua Wade murder trial heard about 40 minutes of testimony Tuesday, squeezed in among hours of protracted recesses and closed-court wrangling among the lawyers.

What they got when Timothy Beckett finally took the stand was a recitation of his criminal resume, including the gang he helped create, the details of his cooperation with police in the Wade case and his subsequent armed-robbery history.

And this was just direct examination. Cross-examination of Beckett is scheduled to begin today.

Beckett, 20, is one of several young men who say Wade told them he beat Della Brown to death then showed them Brown's body before police found it on Sept. 2, 2000, in an abandoned Spenard shed. Wade, Beckett and others had been hanging around an auto-repair shop for a couple of days about a block from the shed.

At first, according to Beckett, he gave Wade advice about covering his tracks so he wouldn't get caught. But a little more than three weeks later, Beckett agreed to wear a police wire and engage Wade in conversation about the murder. The tape, in which Wade appears to admit killing Brown, was played Monday

See Page B-2, WADE

Timothy Beckett testified Tuesday in the trial of Joshua Wade in Anchorage Superior Court.

The defense has pegged Timothy Beckett as a better suspect for the murder than Joshua Wade.

WADE: *Wired informant takes stand*

Continued from B-1

for the jury.

Beckett also collected a $1,000 reward from Crime Stoppers for giving Wade's name to police. He said he shared the money with a friend who helped set up the wired conversation.

The defense has pegged Beckett as a better suspect for the murder than Wade. Defense attorney Jim McComas spent one of the no-jury sessions locking and loading for his assault on Beckett's story, trying to get copies of photographs in federal possession that show Beckett and his pals posing with guns, seeking proof that Beckett was still an active gang leader long after he testified he quit.

McComas won most of his requests but was frustrated at not being able to get a copy of Beckett's federal pre-sentence report. Beckett is awaiting sentencing on federal and state armed robbery convictions.

McComas blamed the prosecution for not trying hard enough to get the report. But prosecutor Mary Anne Henry said the federal court has stonewalled both sides.

"There's not much we can do," she said. Judge Mike Wolverton expressed his displeasure at the feds' unwillingness to cooperate with a state court but refused to order Beckett's lawyer in the federal case to produce his copy of the report.

McComas is looking for evidence that Beckett expects to get a reduced federal sentence in return for his testimony against Wade. His deal with the state says only that his sentence on the state robbery conviction will run at the same time as his federal sentence.

I Just Wanted To Go Fishing !!!

Testimony cuts Beckett's jail time

Timothy Beckett testified in the trial of Joshua Wade for the murder of Della Brown. Wade was acquitted.

■ 35 YEARS: Witness was supposed to serve 61 or 62 years for armed robbery conviction.

By NICOLE TSONG
Anchorage Daily News

Timothy Beckett's testimony may not have helped the state get a conviction in the Joshua Wade murder trial, but his time on the witness stand in February cut his prison time for federal robbery charges by at least 26 years.

A U.S. district judge sentenced Beckett to 35 years in prison Wednesday for multiple counts of armed robbery of the Spenard Motel in January 2001. The 23-year-old originally faced 61 to 62 years after a jury convicted him last May on charges of armed robbery, brandishing a firearm and providing firearms to people who used them in crimes of violence.

Beckett rejected plea bargains offered before his trial, federal prosecutors said, and refused to help investigators with information against members of his gang, Good Boys Trece Sorenos. But because he provided "useful, truthful and complete" testimony at the Wade trial, prosecutors asked the judge to reduce the sentence to a range of 35 to 40 years.

Wade was acquitted last month on charges that he murdered Della Brown.

John Pharr, Beckett's attorney, said the sentence was "Draconian," but an improvement over 61 years.

Federal prosecutors said Beckett helped plan and commit three robberies in January 2001 at the Spenard Motel, brandishing handguns.

U.S. District Judge James Fitzgerald also ordered Beckett to pay restitution of $2,652. He shares that obligation with others convicted in the same robbery spree, the judge said.

Beckett agreed to waive his right to appeal in federal court, contradicting statements made in the Wade trial. When Wade's attorneys accused him of lying to get a deal

See Page B-4, **BECKETT**

BECKETT: *Sentence reduced by at least 26 years*

Continued from B-1

with federal prosecutors, Beckett testified he was wrongfully convicted and was certain the conviction would be thrown out during an appeal.

Kevin Feldis, an assistant U.S. attorney, said there was no agreement with Beckett before Wade's trial. Pharr didn't approach him about a sentence reduction in exchange for the testimony until after the murder trial ended, Feldis said.

Before Wednesday's hearing, Beckett, who often talked tough on the witness stand and sports a tattoo on his neck, waved, grinned and wiggled his eyebrows at his 13-month-old niece as the baby toddled around the courtroom and giggled. But as the judge announced his sentence, he closed his eyes and looked down.

He told Fitzgerald before sentencing that he was ready to spend 35 years in prison.

"I don't agree with it," he said. "But there's nothing you can do."

He apologized.

"They are not choices I would make again in my life," he said.

■ Daily News reporter Nicole Tsong can be reached at ntsong@adn.com or 257-4450.

Chapter 13

Hangin' Wit' My Homefry!

Why I really decided to go visit Gabe is a bit of a mystery to me. Curiosity I guess. Why did he want me to come see him? Well, I guess the first time I went to see him it was because he had found Ray-Ray's grandmother's phone number in the "discovery" papers that all defendants are presented with. I think it is bullshit that phone numbers are included in that stuff. What about protecting the innocent? Why do the criminals (not that I don't think Ray-Ray is a criminal - just not her Grandma) get all the breaks? Anyway, June Something, 2001, I was running the salon reports and waiting for Tiny, when I got a phone call from Ray-Ray who was all sorts of upset because Gabe had called and left a message. They thought that I had given him the phone number. Jeez! Why in the hell would I do that? Would this nightmare never end? It was bad enough that Gabe's gurlfriend called me at home and at work to harass me still. After a heated discussion with Ray-Ray, I determined that after work I would go over to the jail for the first time and talk to him. See what was up. Let him know that she didn't live there anymore. Besides that, I was curious why he even wanted me to come visit in the first place.

So after work I rushed over to the jail here in town with my stomach all in knots only to discover that he had been moved to Palmer. Palmer is a small town a short bit northeast of Anchorage. I wondered why they moved him there. A bit disappointed and relieved at the same time, I drove home and called Officer Ryan to complain about the phone call to Ray's grandma. He is the one who told me about the discovery papers. I am fairly certain that Officer Ryan had other more important things to do besides listen to me complain about such things that might seem trivial now. After all, wasn't the GTS in jail? But what about The Girlfriend? Why was she and the other skanks calling my house to ask about Ray? Was that true harassment? And what about Ray? Why wasn't she in trouble? Every phone call renewed my anger towards her! Shit!.

Anyway, after being assured that all was fine, I forgot about stuff for awhile. Running a salon is a big enough pain in the ass without worrying about those punks. I mean, talk about drama! I actually hired one cute little gal that was so Christian-ified that she felt she had to quit because we carried a line of products that had the words bitch, slut, and sinful on the bottles! She felt that her church clients couldn't handle our "saucy" conversations. That's cool, whatever. Hoochie quit back in June since we couldn't see eye to eye. Not that that mattered anyway, since the House Of Ill Repute where she had been working was definitely rubbing off on her. Lil' Dancer was off taking dancing lessons in New York and wouldn't be back till August, and Schmoozie had been canned. Yep, twas just me and Tiny for a couple of months. I always liked her the best anyway. She is always there although quite cranky if she misses a smoke break. One good thing about that time though, the morning reports didn't take long to run! And we saved alot of money on coffee!

Mary Oyster

That summer I fished every weekend, was on steroids every month, quit breathing on the river, (my Fishing Partner saved me), and because of the steroids my waders got smaller and smaller. What would I do after exploding out of them? I prayed for a cure for asthma, prayed that I wouldn't blow outta my waders, I prayed that I would finish this book, I prayed that Ray-Ray would be normal, and I prayed that the salon wouldn't do down in bankruptcy. If it was going to go down, I wanted it to go down in flames! Heh heh heh... Now that I said that, it will happen just so, and I will be a suspect. So lets just strike that from the record!

One fine drizzly morning while mixing a beautiful red hair color for on of my more favored clients, I decided to go see Gabe in Palmer. He fairly begged me to come. He said that I could have the "discovery" papers if I came. In the papers was the confession of Ray-Ray that she was the GTS leaders girlfriend and some other interesting info that I wanted for this book. So I jumped in my Bronco, placed a picture of his baby in my pocket, popped in a Rob Zombie cd, grabbed coffee and set off for Palmer. I must mention here that I when driving to something important, I secretly pretend that I am driving a black or silver Hummer. Not one of the new SUV types. No, I'm talking a full on massive rig with giant tires, and a winch, and a brush guard, and a truck box. I sure would like that. Whew! Anyway, it is amazing how fast a person can drive when listening to the proper driving music! "In the mouth of madness, I'm demon speeding!", something like that. Man I had a stomach ache. Big Daddy was curious too. Tiny was scared, my Fishing Partner never found out, my kids were excited, Ray-Ray didn't know. Basically, everyone who did know that I was going to visit had an opinion. All expected a phone call upon my return!

So when you drive up there, they have a really slow, curvy road. Then you come to the spot. It wasn't exactly what I expected. I figured to see guards with guns and stuff. All that was there were buildings with high fences topped with tons of razor wire. You check in, spit out your gum, (my favorite is Eclipse brand, yum, yum,) and then you stand around with a few other people who are going to visit their inmate relatives & friends. Then you get in a van after being searched and the van takes you to these buildings. All the times I went there, I was the only one to get out for the maximum secured area. It was nerve wracking at first.

Then the gate opens and you go to stand in front of another door and push a button. Then after ant eternity the door buzzes and you go in to stand in front of another door. Then you get buzzed in again and you put your keys in a metal drawer and sit down in a rather uncomfortable chair. There is a scratched up window looking into the little room where the inmate gets to sit. At the bottom of the glass is a metal deal with holes so that you can hear each other talk. It is kind of dark and you can see where the guard room is and a hall where the cells are. Sometimes you can see a guy walking around doing janitorial. The guy who is doing janitorial always flips Gabe shit when I have visited.

Anyhoo, that first day while making my observations about the Palmer Correctional Facility, out from one of the cells rushed a person. I knew it had to be Gabe, and I wondered what he looked like all healthy. (The last time I had seen him he was his customary yellow, trashed liver color.) It was him! He blasted in, thumped himself on the chest and made a peace sign. The hugest grin I have EVER seen on anyone's face! He was thrilled to see me. He was laughing and had teary eyes. Taken aback by this display, really, I laughed back at him. And then we both said Waaazzuuup! And he said alot of yo's. His hands were shaking and he continuously rolled the bottom of his shirt up and down. "I can't believe you came! You da only one who has came ta see me! My own gurl hasn't even came ta see me. I always knew you was true! Thank you so much! Thank you! Thank you!" I have never seen a more grateful person. Wow.... Plus his healthier lifestyle had most definitely improved his appearance. He still had a clean shaven head and the fag tag. (He hates it when I tell him what *I* think fag tags are for in prison! Yo! They are really a street thing - when a homey gets killed, you grow a tail in memory of that person.)

And all I could say was that of course I came, I had after all promised that I would. *What would Officer Ryan think?* I asked Gabe why he started calling me. I asked him why he wanted to see me. After all, I was the person who he was going to rob and beat up or kill and stuff. I asked him if he remembered all that.

He looked sheepish and said that I should have never listened to the po-lece. He says they are all liar's and he would never have hurt a woman. I asked him if he forgot about the time he told me he cracked his girl in the jaw for doing drugs. He of course remembered that, and said so. His answers for wanting to see me are always the same. He was curious about me and since I was his baby's Granma, we were family. He would do anything for me.

I flipped out the picture of the baby he had never seen. I asked him to hold up his hands to the glass. He declined because he had SOUTHSIDE tattooed one letter at a time on his knuckles. I told him that I didn't care about that, I wanted to see the shape of his hands, you know to compare to the baby picture. He slowly put them up. At first I couldn't look at them because I was staring into his eyes. Not *into* them really but memorizing the shape and color of them which matched the picture. Then I looked at his hands. Yo! They matched my grandsons perfectly as did his eyes. I became emotional for a short minute (very short) and held the photo up to the glass. He stared, mesmerized and then threw himself back in his chair with a loud "Haaaaaaa!" "He's a handsome dude, jus like me!" he exclaimed. Then he jumped up and ran out of the room. I thought "What the heck?!" Then he came running back with a stack of papers and a photo of his nephew. The nephew looked like a blonde version of my grandson. Wow...

The papers he pressed up against the window were part of the discovery papers. My cell phone conversation with him was there. Lots of pages of taped cell phone conversations with Ray-Ray including something saying she knew what being the leaders girlfriend meant. I felt sick and at the same time excited that I had proof that SHE KNEW WHAT SHE WAS INTO. Someone once asked my why I wanted that proof. I just wanted it. Now, it matters not one bit for nothing has changed. You can't change the past.

Then before I knew it my visit was up. A whole hour was gone. Gabe pressed his hands to the window and a whole bunch of thank-you's came out. And then I drove home. I couldn't wait to tell Big Daddy. The weird thing was, I found myself really pitying Gabe. I had better check myself, I figured..........

My last two visits with Gabe were in September 2002. The first one was after he was to be sentenced in his State case. I left the salon and went to the hearing on September 6, 2002 figuring that he was just being sentenced for that same stuff that he had been sentenced federally. What a moron I am! He and his crew had broken into someone's house. Gabe had shoved his gun so far down the guys throat that he choked on his own broken teeth and pissed all over himself. At the same time his friend Crim beat a lady in there so bad that she miscarried a baby. I sat there in the courtroom stunned. Everyone knows what stunned feels like I am sure! I couldn't breath and felt a huge asthma attack threatening to arrive. Gabe looked frantically back at me as he was finger printed. His hideous girlfriend was all smiles for him as she struggled to breathe after a night or a week of heavy cocaine use. She certainly was plugged up anyway. I could go on about that but I won't.

I might as well tell everyone reading this that on that day he could have received 1-20 years for his crimes. There was much discussion about the difference between "serious" crime and "most serious". Gabe had committed "most serious" because:

1. There was danger of loss of life.

2. There were multiple victims.

3. He was a gang leader, and brought his California gang here to Anchorage..

4. The number of people involved that he had control over was quite large..

5. No regard for the safety of people.

The prosecution argued all that stuff and then agreed with the defense that he was quite helpful to the feds. They all talked about how his life in prison was dangerous to him because of the plea bargain and about how he was attacked in jail.

The judge called him a "very scary individual" who was a leader of a dangerous gang in our fair city, with no regard for human life. *My son-in-law! Whew!* But since he was "so cooperative" and his life was in danger and all that, he gave him 8 years on one count and 2 on another. I wrote on my scribbled notes that I was gonna puke. I remember that feeling.

I stood up and motioned him to call me when he got back to Palmer. I knew him well enough now that I could, and wanted to ask him about this "home invasion". That was a Friday. I went to see him on the next Tuesday. Did this crime happen during the time he was living at Ray-Ray's house I wondered? I walked back to the salon in the rain and wished that I was fishing instead. I can fish in the rain all day. Sideways rain, drizzly rain, fat rain, any kind of rain. What the fuck!

Well, since I didn't hear from him except for him to call and say he couldn't talk, I decided to go visit him once again on Tuesday the 10th. Once again the appropriate music choice would either be Rob Zombie or Limp Bizkit for the drive. That way I could get there quickly you know. When I got there, Gabe came out happy as ever except for one gripe that he had. The prison barber had messed his hair buzz up and it looked like a tuft was growing out of the top! Made him look kind of comical. "Yo! Wazzzzuup Mary?" he asked as always. He wanted to know right away if I would cut his hair if he could get it approved. Anyway...

I said, "Yo. I wanna know about what you were sentenced for the other day. That's disgusting. You jammed a gun down someone's throat. Is that what you were gonna do to my husband when you were pissed at me? You tell me that you would have never hurt me or mine because of our family ties, but the fact is that you were going to come to my house. Now tell me why you went to this dudes house! And when exactly was this? Were you living with Ray-Ray? Tell me the truth!" I was pretty worked up. I hadn't been able to shake the visual I had conjured up in my head about Gabe shoving a gun down Big Daddy's throat. I know for a fact that he wouldn't have hesitated to do that and I was rather thankful that I had made friends with him. Officer Ryan and the other po-lece were right. It was definitely a good thing to be friends with him rather than the other way if you know what I mean.

The basic breakdown story of this particular robbery was that the home invasion was done as a retaliation act. The man with the broken teeth and pee running down his legs was the father of one of Gabe's nieces. He supposedly abused the niece and Gabe decided to make him pay. And pay he did with broken teeth and all. There was another person who was beaten as well. The woman who miscarried the baby was just an innocent bystander and Crim beat her and she lost the baby. Gabe was so enraged that Crim hurt that lady that he made him do another robbery. Remember the third Spenard Hotel robbery? You know the one where Crim got shot by the owner? Well, I guess you could say, what comes around goes around. Now, I never figured out the parts all the other GTS crew members, including his brother Ean, played in this deal. Gabe is careful to step around certain issues. He will not talk trash about his own.

Ok. So in Gabe's mind the beatings were completely justified because of abuse to someone he cares about. That is fine. Haven't we all sworn at one time or another if anyone ever hurt our children that we might give it back to the abuser twice as hard? I know I have. I have even thought up horrible tortures to anyone that would possibly hurt my children. But I have never actually known anyone who in fact did do something like that. Plus, then his crew member had to be punished for beating a woman. It's amazing the "code of ethics" and justifications Gabe has. I can see some of them, violent though they are. And what was sick, was that I actually laughed at parts of his story. Have you ever watched that movie "Very Bad Things" with Cameron Diaz? It was like that. Laughing at stuff that should never be funny. Shameful. I just wished that Ray-Ray had never introduced me to someone like that, and once again I was filled with fear. Fear and relief that I had befriended him. He swore up and down that he never planned to hurt us. Only get his dog back. *Ray-Ray, why did you need that dog?*

The next day was September 11, 2002. The anniversary of the World Trade Center bombings. Once again I wasn't thinking about those victims as much as I should. Selfishly, I was thinking about how I was thankful my family was safe from local terrorist punks.

September 14 was to be a festive day at the salon. It was Tiny's birthday and I had bought a cake and balloons. Lil' Dancer was there and we were all busy whipping out fabulous hairdo's and listening to Tiny's plans for a fine date. She was figuring on beautifying herself and having someone take her out to dinner. I had to leave my clients several times during the day because we had no receptionist during that time. There came a "free call" from Cook Inlet Pretrial. I hit the "yes" button and was shocked to hear "Yo. This is Ean. Gabe's brother." *What the fuck!*

Quickly I ducked into the hallway. My heart was beating fast. Why would Timothy Ean Becket be calling me? Not only was he co-leader of the GTS, but he also wore a wire for the upcoming murder trial of Joshua Wade. (Joshua Wade was going to be on trial for murdering Della Brown in September of 2000, and repeatedly raping her body. (A whole other story that I won't get into since I don't know much about it.) How did he get my number? What did he want?

"Hey yo, this is Mary. Wazzzuup?" I asked.

"Yo. Jus wondering how my nephew is. Jus seein' what you are up to. Been meaning to call you and get to know you." He didn't sound half as gangstery as Gabe. Then he wanted to know if I had heard from Gabe. Wanted to let me know that his girlfriend was friends with Gabe's girlfriend and they were both out of jail. *Why did I need to know that?* Shit! Here we go again. I made a mental note that I would kick Ray-Ray's ass should she ever cross my path again.

I figured that now I would have to befriend this guy too. So I filled him in briefly how Ray-Ray was good, her baby was good, and how Gabe was good. That was it. Later I found out that he had contacted a couple of my relatives looking for me. Why does the prison system allow so much access to the phone? I decided to go see Gabe again to see if he knew why his brother was calling me.

I rushed out to Palmer after work leaving Tiny to her beautifying. I made a mental note to get some new music. Rob Zombie and Limp Bizkit were getting old and I was definitely tired of everything else that I had. Plus it wasn't as much fun pretending the Bronco was a Hummer either. Sad. Gabe was surprised to see me. He was expecting his hideous girlfriend. He should have known that she would never come and to this day has still never been to visit him. Anyway, he was crushed that I was mad and truly didn't know why his brother would be calling me or my relatives. In fact, he made all kind of threats against him which he would never be able to pursue due to him being in a different jail and all. Then we talked about the same old shit like the other times and then I left. (That was my last visit with Gabe before he was sent to Seward Correctional.) From there, I decided that I was going to go pay a visit to Ean.

Once in town I cruised over to the jail for my visit. But I was too late. I had myself all worked up for a confrontation for nothing. I didn't want to call the po-lece yet. It wasn't like he really threatened me or anything. They might even laugh at me. Ray-Ray didn't have much to say about the incident either. She also swears that she knew nothing about the upcoming murder trial and still swears to this day that she didn't know how violent her gangster family was/is. How a person doesn't know that kind of stuff about a room full of room-mates is beyond me!

Anyway, that month the calls from Gabe came infrequently as they were much stricter in a real prison. But the calls from Ean increased. He just calls to bullshit and sometimes if I am free, I take the calls. I'm scared of him. I asked him once about wearing the wire for the investigation of Joshua Wade. I also asked him why he went to look at her body. He said that Josh asked him to "help" him with something and then he went with him. That was all he would say. He said that he would tell me anything I want to know if I was to go visit him. Shit! Why do they always want me to come visit? His street name is Romeo.

It is now January 2003, and I still haven't visited him. The Joshua Wade murder trial has finally started. Both Ian and Gabe will be testifying. Ian for the prosecution and Gabe for the defense. Ray-Ray doesn't say much about this. She pretends like nothing happened. Sort of a blank stare I can feel on the end of the phone line. Pretty much what I expected.

Chapter 14

Writings From The Big House!

I started to receive letters from Gabe. Also poems from him and Romeo. I have copied them exactly as they have been written. I have included them in this story to try to show the human side of Gabe. And after talking with him decided that these might actually help a young kid, who possibly might be thinking about being jumped into a gang, to think twice about it.

Letter dated July 30, 2002

Mary, Thank you so much for being here for me. We barely know each other and it seems like you care about me more than a lot of people that have been in my life alot longer, and have even said they loved me. I have not had much in my life but have lived with what I had. I never really had a family but with people like you who needs one. I know I still talk to my biological mother but the thought of having you as a mom has crossed my mind a million times. The thoughts are something like this, "I wonder alot on how if you were mine and my little sisters mom that we probably would not have got adopted as children. Maybe if I had a mother like you I probably would not be here right now. I don't blame my mother going to prison and having me and my sister adopted, or my father abandoning me as a child either for why I am who I am. But I do blame them for starting the building process of who I have become. Don't get me wrong, I love and worship my mother cause I know she loves me and is trying to make up foe everything. I even love my father and I've only talked to him 4 times my whole life but never in person. What surprises me is how I need love and people to care for me, and I know this sounds strange, but, I don't care if I spend the rest of my life in prison as long as I have a person like you in my life. It's crazy how you show me respect and crazy emotions when the only real thing you know about me is my street mentality and corrupt mind. I mean at first that's all you know of me and I know you had this stereotype about me but you took a chance. Well I am hoping that you see J am a good person in my heart and brain and have a feeling you are looking over my bad past and can see I am a person in need of caring people. I don't like to admit that I need some type of friendship caring cause I don't need sympathy, but I am not afraid to admit that I am no gangster and was very stupid in my past. I'm very sorry for messing up mine and Ray-Ray's relationship and me and you could not meet on different terms but I want you to know I have already put my trust in you. When I saw you cry during our visit I knew a <u>real</u> person was sitting in front of me and the most caring person. I love (baby's name) and I love <u>Ray-Ray</u>. I know that may sound weird but I do and wish me and Ray-Ray would never have split up. I see now she was trying to help me and if I would of been mature and smart I would of let her get me off the streets. Tell her sorry and I love her. I know you are my baby's grandma but I love you in a son to mother way. I was so happy when you came to visit. I'm very lonely and have been all my life. Look, I've never been able to trust nobody but my baby sister and that's because me and her have been through everything and more than you can think of and I know she will never leave me in the dust. Do you understand I am trying to let you know I <u>trust you</u> Mary, you are a very good woman and I will never betray you in any way. Look I'm already attached to you cause you show that you care and are my babies grandma, and ther's something about you I truly respect. If you can't handle me being attached to you in a son to mother way, let me know before I get too attached and get hurt if you decide to give up. But if you don't mind you are stuck with me. (smiley face) I don't mind. I've never told nobody, but I want to tell you something very important. I'll tell you when you visit again. I love (baby's name) with all my heart. I do got one you know. I love Ray-Ray too.

Your friend and Grandson's Father,
Gabriel Clark-Aigner

Letter dated August 6, 2002

Mary, What up, I'm just anxious and ready to start my time. Here is a picture I drew for you. I figured that it would be an appropriate one. I rushed through it and I'm sorry if its a little sloppy. Well my mom called my attorney and gave me a new number for me to call. (his mom's number) Guess who else called me ex-bitch R. (girlfriend). That pissed me off. I still love her but I hate her cause she fucked with my emotions. She is a stripper in Showboat in Fairbanks. She is such a ho. She does not know we are not together but she will find out. To tell you the truth I never really felt like anyone cared for me but my baby sister till I really got to meet you. Well the big day is tomorrow and that's when my life will flash before my eyes. Please believe me Mary, but I am sorry for the crimes I have committed to get me where I am now. I am happy I am in jail cause I found God, really realize who I am, and found you, and made (baby's name). Oh yeah, I also would of (???) your receptionist. She does not know it yet but she loves me! Ha ha! I'm just kidding. Hey I appreciate everything and know what you give is not fake. Mary, where have you been all my life? (smiley face) Well I have not got your letter yet, probably will tonight. I will write you another one. If you can, can you send me some lined paper? Well write back.

Your Friend and Grandson's Father

Gabriel Clark Aigner

I did send some lined paper and a Low-rider magazine.

Letter dated September 15, 2002

Hey Mary, I was thinking about my childhood and your kids popped into my head. I would give anything in the world to have what they have. I wonder how my life would have turned out if I had parents like they do. As much as I want parents like you and your husband I sure did turn out to be a failure to (baby's name). I love him to death. I cry just thinking how much I failed him. Well I will do my best and I will be there for him. I will just leave it to Gangster Granny to get Ray-Ray to let me be a part of (my son's) life. Well I wrote a poem for your kids. It's little way of telling them what my home is like and how lonely I am in my cell. My cell is my home. Believe it or not, since it's really all I have with the stuff inside it, I'm kind of protective about it and get a little violated when people look in or go in it. Well Mary, here is a letter to them also. Maybe you can put the poem or picture on your office wall.

Gabriel

I Just Wanted To Go Fishing !!!

Letter to my kids dated September 15, 2002

Hey you guys are family because of my son. But even if you weren't I would still write to you. Look you two are very lucky to have a good home and people to love you, I would give anything to have what you have now, when I was a kid. I don't blame anyone but myself for where I am at, but I blame my needs and wants. My parents started my criminal life and I decided to keep it up. I never had a home or even good parents. Lucky for me my mother is trying to make up for the past. Most people with lives like mine never get that chance. From what your mother says about you two during our visits, you guys are smart and loving and very important to her. I'm sorry if you guys were scared at first but I would never try to hurt my sons family. Believe it or not I have one of the biggest hearts and am a really nice guy. You know what? Your mom makes me feel more loved than my own mom. I look at you mom as a mom also. I miss Ray-Ray and am sorry for not listening to her. I pray you two will never be bad. Just remember where I ended up. 25 years to serve in prison. All the parties were fun but I guarantee they were not worth what I have to serve. I could go on and on but will save you the lecture. I do know this, I've learned from my mistakes and now all I want is to be as much a father as I can. Keep on being good to your parents and please never go to jail.

Your friend and nephews father,

Gabriel Clark-Aigner

ps. I sent a poem to your mom, so read it if you want. I wrote the poem thinking of you two. It's a poem about my cell, which is my home, and all that I own.

Poem by Gabriel Clark-Aigner dated September 15, 2002

Mary Oyster

My Castle

A man's house is his castle, or so I've heard tell.
Well if such is the case, my castle's a cell.

So alone in my castle I sit on my throne,
And gaze all around at the treasures I own.

A broom and a trash sack, to keep the place clean.
A Walkman radio, that really sounds mean.
An old pair of shades, to cover my eyes.
A couple of towels, and a pair of Levi's.
A handful of letters from a girl I once knew.
My razor and toothbrush, some soap and shampoo.
Some paper and envelopes, and a cheap paper-mate.
Oh yeah, and my sneakers I stole from the state.

There's a half dozen pictures propped up on my shelf,
But since know one visits their all of myself.

There's a couple of headbands, and a watch to tell time,
It blows me away that all this is mine.

That throne that I mentioned, is pure stainless steel,
And at four in the morning that's a hell of a chill.

There's a smidgeon of coffee, and a few packs of smokes,
If this is my castle, it's a pretty poor joke.

I Just Wanted To Go Fishing !!!

A man's home is his castle, or so I've heard tell.
Well, you can have mine, and give me a hotel.

From: Your nephews father and a friend,
Gabriel Clark-Aigner

Letter to Ray-Ray dated September 16, 2002

Ray-Ray, Hey, I know you don't want to hear from me or even like me, but I just want to say I am sorry for not listening to you and not letting you get me off the streets. Look at me now. I'm a failure to our son. I sit in a cell 23 hours a day and most of the time I think about what could have been. When I think of how much I have failed our son (baby's name) I cry. I promise you I am not lying to you. I'm sorry for being stupid when we were together. If I could I would love to go back and change my ways, especially the way I acted towards you. If I would of just slowed down, listened to you, respected you, I would of been there when (baby's name) was born.

I am sorry I was not there when you needed me. Please let me call you and be a part of (baby's name) life. Look, I have nothing anymore. It is sad that the only person who shows me any love is someone else's mom. Your mother. Your mother is the only one I call and the only one who visits. I know she loves and cares for you at least from our conversations we have. I wish I would have realized what a good person you were for me when we first met. I also with that I thought the way I do now. Look, please forgive me and let me be a part of (baby's name) life. Like I said, I am very sorry for everything I have put you through.

Gabriel

  * *She asked me not to send her any letters after the first one, because it caused*

some tension between her new boyfriend and her. They have since broken up and so I figured that I could print it. That and Gabe has given his permission

** *There were a couple of more letters that said pretty much the same. Asking for forgiveness and to be a father. I tell him that someday when the baby is old enough, I will tell him about his father. I also tell him that with the letters and poems, that maybe some good will come out of this. That maybe his son will understand and stay away from bad people. That I think his son will forgive him for not being around as a father figure, and that his gift as a father is loving him enough to let him go.*

Poem By Gabriel Clark-Aigner dated 09/22/02

I Forgive You Mom

At least you are nothing like my father,
Who did not give a fuck or even bother.

Everybody messes up in their past,
I forgive you Mom, it all just happened so fast.

While Jessy and I sit on the floor and play,
The police came and took you away.

You asked them if you can take us to the neighbor,
The man was nice enough to oblige you the favor.

You said your goodbye's and said it's ok,

I Just Wanted To Go Fishing !!!

Gabby go in the room with Jessy and play.

I asked you if you wanted me to shoot him with my toy gun,
You just smiled with a tear and said, "He won't hurt me hun."

I did not know what was happening at first,
But when I realized, the tears came with a burst.

The neighbor tried to block the window,
And what I saw hit me with big blow.

The man had her in cuffs, taking my mom away!
Why wouldn't they just leave her alone, and let her stay?

As they were driving away my heart ached and I missed her,
And instantly thought it's just me and my sister.

I went back to my sister and saw in her eyes,
A scared little girl with nothing but why's.

I went to the floor and gave her a hug,
Ten minutes later asleep on the rug.

At twenty years old I still remember that day,
On my prison cell bunk, I write this poem as I lay.

Gabriel Clark-Aigner

Mary Oyster
Poem by Gabriel Clark-Aigner dated 09/21/02

Dedicated To My Dad "Larry Becket"

Fuck you Dad, you ain't shit to me,
Cause when I was born you decided to flee.

No father to raise me, no mother to care,
A life so insane but not very rare.

How does it feel not to know your youngest son,
But most of all , my life's safari you begun.

Fuck you Dad, you ain't shit to me,
It's your punk ass that started my life's history.

Are you proud of what your son has become?
At age eight, my first experience with shooting a gun.

Throughout my life I could have used your love,
But the description of coward fits you like a glove.

I've shed tears when a friend has died on the street,
But I would not cry if you died at my feet.

I heard you came to Alaska and testified in court,
It's nice to know you give one of your son's support.

How did it feel, you could only tell the jury you don't know me,
That Ean was your life, and that you are a phony.

Did you even know you are a grandfather,
Of course not, why would you bother?

Unlike you I'm proud of my son,
Even in my shameful situation I won't run.

I admit, I was not there when he was born,
And for that my heart is torn.

I'm going to try as much as possible to be in the life of my boy,
And hopefully his life I did not destroy.

Gabriel Clark-Aigner

Note For You Dad - 09/21/02 By Gabriel Clark-Aigner

I sit here writing this poem and for a minute wondered if I was being a hypocrite. Well we are two different people with two different motives. You are a coward and ran by choice. Me, The Man put me behind bars, and that separated me from my son. If I was free, I would be with my son now. I would get on my hands and knees in front of a million people and beg her to give me another chance. Dad, there is more to the story of me and my son's mother but that is none of your fucking business. I will let you know this, she is nothing like my mother and we split up because of my immaturity and non-caring attitude. You were just a coward and left as soon as I was born. At least I realize my mistakes as soon as my son was

Mary Oyster

born. And I will do whatever it takes to be a part of his life as much as I can. Dad, I thank you for one thing, and that's you taught me a lesson. I will not abandon my son and unlike you, let him know that it's not his fault I'm in prison, that I love him and care for him. I'm going to do what I can to get out early enough to bring him to school. All I do now is pray that me, his mother, and our son have a future together. Oh yeah, it's also sorry that my baby's grandma see's you in person before I do. Just so you know, you are dead to me and no longer a part of me.

Poem By Romeo - Written sometime in November 2002

Our Lords Love & Glory

The pain in my heart is all I feel,
And it's your love that made it real,
Lord, you're the only one that can make it heal.

For you are the mighty God, who stands and rules with your glorious rode.

I try not to forget the strength your love brings,
But right now all I can feel is the devils sting.

Jesus you are my lord and king,
So please help me beat the devils strings.

Your mercy brings me to each day,
And it's your love that takes me out of dismay.

I love you lord for my life,

Even though I no longer have a wife.

Lord it's your love that brings us glory,

But it's only because of your life story.

I praise you with each body part,

And Lord I love you with all my heart.

Romeo - November, 2002

Poem By Romeo - Written sometime in November, 2002

Your Love

These tears in my eyes,

Are only because I realize,

All the pain that your love brings,

I know that love stings,

But who needs all these strings?

I sit in a cage,

And try to battle all this rage.

When you took all your love away,

You made the pain and brought the rain,

That I see all day,

Mary Oyster

I'm in so much dismay because you took your love away.
So all I do is pray that you'll stay.

I now realize that it was your love that had me hypnotized,
But when you left I was paralyzed.

You have the cure that will make my heart pure.

So God please take this rage,
And let me out of my cage,
So that my life can go to the next stage.

    Romeo - November, 2002

Ode To Gangster Granny

Salon drama, Family trauma
Gangsta's runnin' around.

Gabe's writin' poems, Ean's on the phone
And the big one's swimming away.

Teeny Tiny, Hoochie Mama
Prancing Dancing girl.

Gangster Granny's Fish Mobile
It's the happy fishing car!

I Just Wanted To Go Fishing !!!

She just wanted to go fishin'
On the banks of the Anchor River sandbar.

Ray-Ray's prego by the local gangsta and
Wrinkle eaten, Lay Riverman down.

It's 12:00! It's fishin' time
Load up the Mobile it's time to go.

Gangster Granny wants to fish at
The grassy fishin' hole!

Little did she know the trouble
She'd get into by grabbin'
Gabe by the ear!

Kickin' him out of the rank smellin' house
Put the litter-box by the window sill.

by: Marthalicious!

Mary Oyster

Chapter 15

Yo! Da End Of Da Story

Ray-Ray has become a rather self righteous person who is finally using her schooling. She works in a huge salon in another state and digs being a mom. Very cool turn-around. She still hasn't acknowledged to anyone her gangster lifestyle *choice*. She has apologized however for causing everyone pain for "everything". She also never did her time for shoplifting at two stores here which was ten days or eighty hours of community service. I still think that she should have done some sort of time just for having a violent gang living at her house. She did pay a big price I guess though - she lost her own home, lost multiple jobs and cars, she lost her pets, and most of all, the trust and respect of her natural family. Shit, her brother and sister don't care if they ever see her again. As far as Big Daddy, I don't know what he thinks. He's not much of a talker.

As for me, I wish my retarded clients would quit asking me how I like being a grandma! How in the hell would I know? She took that from me. Maybe someday........

Gabe is in a federal prison in California. He still calls the salon every week. He likes it there way better than regular jail because he gets to be in the open population hangin' with his new homey's. He says that I am not to be afraid of Romeo. He says that Ean is nothing but a punk-ass, and says that he is full of shit that he has people outside of jail that will answer his beck and call. (I told Gabe I was afraid of him.) I haven't decided if I believe that. I feel bad for the circumstances of his upbringing and wish I could take care of all the other children that are neglected so that they don't grow up mean and hateful. His adopted mother told me about all the therapy and anger management sessions he had as a child. As a child he never had a chance - he was born addicted to a substance of some sort (why his mother was allowed to give birth to four children is beyond me). Do I think he can be rehabilitated? Rehabilitated? Love that word! Hmm... I don't think he will be able to function as a productive person in the community. He knows nothing but gang and prison life. At the same time, I am no longer afraid of him. He says I am the only one he trusts. Sad. Has he read this book? Yes, and he thought it funny.

Ean (Romeo) is still here awaiting transfer to a federal prison. He was sentenced to thirty five years on May 14, 2003. He still phones the salon once in awhile, just like Gabe. He fills me in on important information like saying it was him that organized the crew to "roll on over" to Ray-Ray's house to see "what-up" the day I Was Chillin' Wit Da Feds. He also mentioned that he told them not to shoot me. That particular festivity might come later. He testified in the Joshua Wade (found not guilty) murder trial that Josh took him to the house to see the body of Della Brown. The defense says Ean committed the murder. Gabe insists that I shouldn't be afraid of him, and says that he is a "punk-ass". I swear that if he was the star in a horror flick, maggots would crawl outta his mouth between his black rotten teeth. Because of his teeth, I never figured out how he became

Romeo! I shall never know. I do know that he makes Gabe look like Mel Gibson. At least in photo's. Officer Ryan says that I don't need to worry about him so I guess I won't.

Capone is still running around gangbanging. I used to see him across the street from the salon once in awhile. He hugged me twice and ran off. Both times he had something under his jacket that he was protecting. Either a gun or drugs. I dunno.

The gurlz are all laying low. Trying to stay out of trouble I reckon. Who knows? I wonder if they will ever get their teeth fixed. I wonder if they're raising good gangster babies and if they dress them in blue. One would hope that they will at least teach them to fold their rags in proper GTS fashion! Make all the daddies proud!

Tiny is still with me at the salon, and will be until the ship does down which will be soon! When it does go down, she would like to purchase it for a penny or two. She still must beautify herself daily for dates because she is too neurotic to keep a man if she does ever pick one. And what a decision it will be since there is quite a bevy of loyal followers!

Lil' Dancer scored herself a dancing contract on a cruise ship. So she is off dancing around the world and will be back sometime in 2003. She decided that music videos weren't really her thing.

Hoochie went on to become a low rent chop-shop stylist. 'Twas more her style which is cool if that is your thing. Whether or not she still works at a house of ill repute is anyone's guess.

Big Daddy is building houses and training dogs. Now that he doesn't have to worry about gangsters and stuff, he has time for that sort of thing. I have never told him that Romeo calls me all the time. I didn't want him to flare his nose all out of whack and worry. In fact, he doesn't get why I am so interested in the murder trial proceedings, and says that Romeo has nothing to do with this story. He must have forgotten that the gurlz said Romeo was the one who ordered the crew to threaten to blow up Ra-Ray's house on Gabe's behalf. You remember, the day I was just supposed to go fishing? That day. Well, I guess if this gets published he'll find out!

Bunky and The Jumble Master are genius kids who strive to do well in school. They have possibly forgiven Ray-Ray for their perception of abandonment. I don't know. I do know that they will never turn to the gangster way although they love gangsta music! Hip-hop actually. They never got into rock-n-roll! They get tired of listening to me tirade about gangsters and other hoodlums. I probably should lay off a bit.

Daizy is busy getting the word out that she wants to be a parole officer. Cool. Her fishing skills have improved immensely and she still digs midnight runs to the fishing hole, although she has cooled her enthusiasm for my driving. She has sworn to perfect her cast this year.

My Fishing Partner is trying to ditch me in favor for duck hunting with Big Daddy. Actually he has grown tired of babysitting me during my frequent asthma attacks on the river. I have assured him that I have been cured and won't be a problem this season. Because I have fibbed to him about being cured, (which maybe I am), he has come up with a new tradition for King season other than flipping me constant shit (if he isn't giving me an extremely hard time, I take offense because that can only mean that he is disgusted with me). We will start fishing for kings at midnight like always, and we wont stop until it closes at midnight four weeks later. Sounds good huh!

Officer Ryan is hopefully still here in Anchorage busting gangsters and other criminals. If this book gets published, I will give him the first copy. I have told him about this story and of course he found it humorous. I also wrote a letter to

I Just Wanted To Go Fishing !!!

the editor about gangsters and thanked him. (Our news paper up here refuses to do a story on the gang problem here - I repeatedly asked them to.) Anyway, the po-leece rule!!!!! Some of them even get their hair done at Mercury. I should have a free cop hair day for my appreciation. I'll have to ask the girls (not gurlz) about that.

Mercury Studio is still there on the corner of the mall across from Nordstrom's. Since this story started it has seen several receptionists come and go. We have a huge lawsuit against us from a psychotic wanna-be receptionist, which is another story. Tiny's best friend Marthalicious, is our Saturday receptionist and she is writing a hilarious song about this book. We have seen a couple of stylists come and go, sorta like the receptionists. Right now we have a new crazy stylist from the Lower 48 who is a fine gospel singer as well as a great newscaster hairstylist.. She plans to one day be the lead singer of a Christian rock band! She's sort of a Holy Roller who probably smokes the Lord's herb and drinks of the Lords vine, and we all love her anyway! She even talks to Gabe on the phone for her afternoon amusement at the salon. We are all still broke but that's gonna change! Now that all the gangster bullshit is over (I think), I can concentrate on being a good employer and hairstylist. Maybe renegotiate my ridiculous lease. Maybe sell the salon! Hey! Now that's an idea! Yeah, that's what I will do! *Maybe Tiny really does want to buy it.* I would cut her one helluva deal!

I'll tell ya what though, I really want to be a gangster busting cop. If only I wasn't so freakin' fat (8,000 lbs overweight) and so old (40), and if only I didn't have asthma. You can't exactly chase down the little bastards if you can't breathe.

Anyway, the end of the story is this: It will never be over for me because of the obvious family connections! I will always wonder what society can do to prevent this shit. If I couldn't do it at home for my own kid, how will the rest of us do it for the kids whose parents don't even give a shit about *their* kids? And what about all the kids that are raised *in* gangs? I wonder that since there is such a big problem up here in Small Town Alaska, how big is the problem in the Lower 48? *If the gangs have so many "rights" and the cops have less authority to do their jobs, how will this problem ever end?* Everyone can say that it begins at home, this is true enough, but where does it end? I certainly don't know. I'll tell ya what else, I sleep with my gun now when Big Daddy is out of town. Just like Gabe did. And I'll tell ya another thing, if a fucking gangster comes into my house, I'll shoot first and ask questions later! Aw-rite? Tha's right.

That is all I have to say. And now I am signing off! Maybe get my fishing gear together! Yeah, that sounds good. Sounds really good! Maybe give Daizy a call for a Power Run. The day all this started, I JUST WANTED TO GO FISHING!!!!! And now I can.

Yo! Gangster Granny! Yo! Peace out.

The End

ps. If this book becomes famous and a movie gets made out of it, then I shall ask Eminem to play Gabe, (except that Eminem is WAY cuter than my son-in-law), or maybe just write a rap tune for the sound track. I don't know who would play me because it is hard to teach people to catch salmon properly. And Gangster Granny would definitely be driving a real Hummer in the movie. I don't care what anyone says, Hummers rule! Now for sure I gotta go! And goodbye! Yo!

About The Author

Mary Oyster is a hairstylist in Anchorage, Alaska who moved there in 1983 from Colorado where she had been a fishin' fool her entire life. After discovering the Fish Panic of Alaskan streams, she decided to stay on and raise a family and catch lots of fish! This is her first written book, and only the person who lived this story could possibly write it!

Printed in the United States
16197LVS00007B/295-324